Beyond the Dream

Ira Berkow

Beyond the Dream

Occasional Heroes of Sports

Foreword by Red Smith

Atheneum New York *1975*

LIBRARY OF CONGRESS CATALOGING IN PUBLICATION DATA
Berkow, Ira. Beyond the Dream: Occasional Heroes of Sports.
SUMMARY: Brief biographical sketches of personalities from every aspect of sports.
1. Athletes–Biography–Juvenile literature.
2. Sports–Biography–Juvenile literature.
[1. Athletes. 2. Sports–Biography] I. Title.
GV697.A1B47 796'.092'2 [B] 75–16761
ISBN 0–689–30489–7

Published simultaneously in Canada by McClelland & Stewart, Ltd.
Manufactured in the United States of America by H. Wolff, New York
Designed by Harry Ford
First Edition

For Wally Allen, Dave Burgin and Murray Olderman,
starting blocks

Acknowledgments to Ralph Novak, Ross Gelbspan, Ernestine Guglielmo, Joyce Gabriel, Don Graff, Bob Cochnar, Boyd Lewis, Bob Metz, Marty Ralbovsky, Ann Sanger, Hana Umlauf and Nancy Pratt.

Foreword by Red Smith

The tale goes that a father took his Little League son to Shea Stadium to show how big leaguers played the game. In the seventh inning the kid asked, "When do the daddies run out on the field and holler at the umpire?" If this seems a faintly bitter joke, read Ira Berkow's story about Fiore Tenace, whose nagging about the way his son played baseball put the boy in hospital with an ulcer at the age of thirteen.

Gene Tenace's father had his way, for at twenty-six the son became a World Series star. We can only imagine what price Gene had to pay, what agonies of heartburn he endured to bring vicarious fulfillment to a cruelly selfish man whose own baseball ambitions had been thwarted. The beauty of Ira Berkow's reporting is that he does not describe Fiore Tenace as selfish or unfeeling. He just tells the story in the words of Gene's mother and lets the reader compare Fiore with those blood-curdling Hollywood mothers clawing for film stardom for their toddlers.

I am proud of Ira Berkow. We became friends by mail when he was an undergraduate writing sports for his college newspaper. He sent samples of his work for criticism, and I am pretty sure I responded with free advice, yet in spite of this he became sports editor of Newspaper Enterprise Service.

It can be stated as a law that the sportswriter whose horizons are no wider than the outfield fences is a bad sportswriter, because he has no sense of proportion and no awareness of the real world around him. Ira Berkow knows that what is important about a game is not the score but the people who play it.

He gets inside people—the college wrestler who feels failure after winning 171 matches; Dave Cowens, a professional basketball player living alone in the woods like Thoreau on Walden Pond; the football player at Marshall University who was not on the plane that crashed with seventy-five of his teammates, coaches and friends; the boxer from the North of Ireland who dodged bombs and bullets to get to the Olympics; Chris Evert, a pig-tailed princess suddenly hearing herself booed; and the kid from Binger, Oklahoma, whose valedictory address at high school commencement was entitled, "How the Youth of Today Will Be the Leaders of the Next Generation." His name is Johnny Bench.

I read Ira, the professional, and remember our first meeting at a World Series game that he attended with a classmate while still in college. Didn't writing about games every day grow dreadfully dull, the classmate asked. Only to dull minds, I told him, and I tried to explain that in newspaper work, unlike the wholesale hardware game, today was always different from yesterday and tomorrow refreshingly different from today.

I don't think I made the point effectively, but Ira does. Read the pieces that follow, and you will know what I meant.

Introduction

Three hundred and seventy years later, Shakespeare might have written: "All the world's a ball field, and all the men and women merely players." For sport today appears to be the recreation for the masses that the stage was in Elizabethan England.

Shakespeare added that one man in his time plays many parts, "his acts being seven ages."

The life of the athlete may also be seen in seven ages, from Little Leaguer tottering under the load of bat and parent, through schoolboy sports, into his shaky early years, his seasons of heady pride, then his maturing, questioning days, the waning moments when he clings to his job like a wet sweatshirt, and, finally, the withered, white-haired codger who may be found dozing on his scrapbook.

Most of those ages, in one way or another, are represented in the following pages.

The stories derive from my columns for Newspaper Enterprise Association over the last seven years. As a columnist for a national feature service, my job was to be more concerned with the players than with the scores.

Since I was writing with a week or more time span between when the piece was kicked out of the typewriter and when it landed in the hands of the 700 or so NEA newspaper clients, I had to seek the "angle" that might hold up for a reasonable length of time.

Also, I had wide latitude in subject matter, mood and view.

So the pieces here are broadly singular, and reflect little more than one man's interests and sniffings.

Ira Berkow

New York City, February 1975

Contents

Youngbloods

Prime Time

A Few Kicks Left

Beyond the Rainbow

The Sidelines' Other Side

Youngbloods

The smell of the ball to the young athlete is intoxicating, like his dreams of glory.

Roberto Clemente's Legacy

San Juan, Puerto Rico, February, 1974

Except for the threat that always lurks of a brief outburst of tropical rain, it was a glorious day.

Bright kites soared in the blue sky. On the green ballfield below, a high school band, all tasseled, high hatted and white booted, practiced a merengue to the beat of a drum, the toot of a whistle, and the perky tinkle of a xylophone. In more serious matters, Little Leaguers warmed up by tossing and chasing baseballs and baseball caps.

And soon, the highlight of this sun-splashed February morning: Mrs. Vera Clemente was scheduled to throw out the first ball of the official opening of the new Roberto Clemente Little League in the old quarter of San Juan.

Members of the nine teams were assembling. One 11-year-old center fielder wearing a floppy Dodgers uniform carried a tube of Ben-Gay in his back pocket. He explained that the ointment made his throwing arm feel good.

Nearby, leaning against a palm tree as he slipped on spikes, was Angel Ramos, the brightly smiling umpire. "I grew up with Roberto in a barrio in Carolina," he said. Carolina is a small town just west of San Juan. "I remember we were on a baseball team together. He was 13 years old, and he did not play much. We say it is 'eating bench.' This is very bad, to 'eat bench.' People fight when you say it to them. But one day Roberto was called to bat and he hit a double. From then on, it was 'Roberto, Roberto, Roberto.' "

The location of the ballfield in the Old San Juan is beside El Morro fortress, a 16th-century battlement that kept Corsairs from invading the island. Today, the fortress holds back only the sparkling waves of the Atlantic Ocean.

It was into this ocean that Roberto Clemente's plane vanished shortly after takeoff, two years before, on New Year's Eve, 1972. Clemente was taking food and clothes he had collected to Nicaragua, where he had once played winter ball, and which had just suffered a devastating earthquake.

For days after the plane fell, Vera Clemente walked the beaches searching for a sign of her husband.

Angel Ramos, the umpire, was asked if anything was ever found.

"*Nunca*," he said, "not even a shoe."

Why?

"The sharks," he said.

Angel Ramos told how a wreath had later been placed on the waters where the plane went under. "And the wreath disappears soon too," he said.

It was getting into midmorning, and Mrs. Clemente still had not arrived at the ballfield.

Most of the boys on the nine teams of the Roberto Clemente Little League of the Old San Juan knew the Pittsburgh Pirates Hall-of-Fame outfielder personally. He often organized baseball clinics where he taught them the finer points of the game.

What did they learn? Angel Ramos called over his young nephew Ricky, and asked him. "*Cogelo suave*," replied Ricky. The phrase is Spanish slang for "keep cool." Ricky adds, "He tells us always to get along with teammates, and when we lose, not to fight with someone. The most important thing is fun of competition."

Clemente had long been a popular figure on the island. He was more than just a countryman who brought pride because he had become a famous baseball player. "He grew up poor and he died trying to help the poor," said Ricky.

Before he died, Clemente was working to realize a dream of his, a sports city for Puerto Rican youth. It would house about 1,500 boys and girls who would get expert instruction not only in sports but also in crafts. "Roberto," said Angel Ramos, "felt such activities could help unite humanity."

As the Little Leaguers lined up along the foul lines for the opening ceremonies, one notices that no number 21 was worn. "No one in Puerto Rico is allowed number 21, Roberto's number," explained Angel Ramos. "It is out of national respect."

The ceremonies began without Mrs. Vera Clemente. Sponsors of the teams were introduced. Polite applause. The lady with sequined glasses who was translating the Little League rules from English into Spanish was introduced. A painting showing Roberto Clemente's strong, dark face on a baseball in heaven was given to Mrs. Clemente's stand-in, the secretary of the Clemente Sports City project. She bit her lip to hold back tears.

There had been no stir when it was announced that Vera Clemente would not come this day. It seemed that all understood. She had been under great strain. "Everywhere," explained Luis Mayoral, a Sports City official, "it is 'Roberto, Roberto, Roberto.' " He related how she must go to Pittsburgh to arrange exhibition games with major league teams in San Juan. She goes to Cooperstown. She helps filmmakers on a Roberto picture, spends time with magazine writers and book authors, attends dinners to raise Sports City money, and sifts requests for appearances.

"She has long had the virus, maybe for three months," said Luis Mayoral. "But mostly it is the end of the year and the remembrances of Roberto. So Vera, she is in a depression during the holiday season. And she knows that she must spend more time with the children, Robertito, who is 8, Luisita, 7, and Enrique, 4. For a long time they were like in a vacuum, especially Robertito, who understands best what happened.

"They only have one mommy and one daddy and they need a great deal of mommy now. She has done all this with the marvel of a champion—breathtaking. And I think the family has finally defeated this past year."

The band again struck up a merengue in the infield dust. Kites bobbed in the sky. The ocean rolled against the thick fortress. And a baseball game was about to begin in the new Roberto Clemente Little League in the Old San Juan.

Gene Tenace: No Kid's Game

November, 1972

One day when Gene Tenace was 13 years old, he suffered a stomach spasm and was rushed to a hospital.

His physical problem was diagnosed as an unusually large ulcer. After discussions with Gene, the doctor called in the young patient's mother, Mrs. Ethel Tenace.

"The doctor said Gene's problem came from being preached at so much by his father into becoming a ballplayer," recalled Mrs. Tenace in her house on Route 2, Lucasville, Ohio. "The doctor said that for a child to be so young and have such a bad ulcer was an awful thing.

"Ever since the day Gene was born his father wanted him to be a major league baseball player."

Gene Tenace did indeed become a major leaguer, as well as a batting star of the 1972 World Series.

When Gene Tenace was a Little Leaguer, his father, Fiore, would scold him in front of the entire crowd if the youngster struck out or made a mindless play in the field.

"He would especially cuss Gene out if he didn't swing at a third strike," said Mrs. Tenace. "A boy at that age has fearings. Gene would just stand there and take it. I remember tears would run down his cheeks.

" 'Didn't I always tell you to swing at a third strike? How come you didn't swing?' his father used to scream. Gene, he didn't say anything except, 'I don't know.' If Gene would ever attack back at his father he probably would've got a slap across the mouth. His father used to say, 'No kid who lives under my roof is goin' to sass me.'

"I would holler at his father. 'Leave him alone, he's doing the BEST he could.' But his father used to say, 'If he's going to be a ballplayer he'll do as I say.' "

For one year, at age 13, Gene had to stay out of school and was given a private tutor. He could not play ball. In fact, he could play for only limited periods of time with other children.

"His nerves were so bad," said Mrs. Tenace, "that only once every couple days could he have maybe two children come in and sit with him. They'd play maybe checkers or some games like that. Then they'd have to leave. You see, he'd be gettin' excited and his ulcer would flare up."

Gene was put on a strict diet for one year. "No greasy foods, no salt, no acids, but plenty of ice cream, jello and cottage cheese. Gene didn't like cottage cheese much," she said.

"I've always cooked lasagna and spaghetti and all the Italian dishes. But Gene couldn't eat any of it, and he loved those foods. So I fixed his meal first, then I sent him into the living room. Then the rest of us ate. But I didn't want Gene to be there when we was all eatin'. He'd smell that food. I know what that woulda done to him."

Gene played no ball that year. When he began playing again, the doctor suggested that Fiore Tenace not go to the games. "He stayed away for a couple or three months," said Mrs. Tenace. "Gene always wanted me to come to his ball game. But he asked me to tell Dad not to come because it made him nervous. The doctor said Gene shouldn't play catcher, that goin' up and down would hurt nis stomach. So that's how Gene learned to play all them other positions."

Fiore Tenace had wanted to become a major league baseball player, too. But he suffered an injury when he was 15 years old—a bat swung accidentally by someone cracked him in the base of the skull—and he feels that that stunted his athletic progress. He was the son of a Pennsylvania coal miner who was killed in a mine cave-in when Fiore was nine years old. At 16, Fiore quit school and went to work in the mines. In 1939, at age 18, he joined the Merchant Marine, then entered the Navy when World War II broke out. He also served in the Korean War and was stationed in Philadelphia when Gene was four years old.

Afterward, he became a laborer in southern Ohio, doing everything from ditch-digging to working on high-rise buildings. He is currently a truck driver or, as Mrs. Tenace says, "a teamster."

The Tenaces have one other living child, Nadine, 28. Another daughter, Serena Kay, was killed in an auto accident four years ago at age 21.

Fiore was a semipro player around the Ohio-Pennsylvania area. Gene was often the batboy on his teams. As time went on, Gene was able to give his father some of his own medicine.

"Gene used to holler, 'Why didn't you strike at the ball, dad?' Or something like that," said Mrs. Tenace, laughing. "His dad used to strike out a lot, too. But his dad never took it as sassin'. He just figured Gene was hollerin' to hear himself holler at the ballpark.

"Gene was afraid of his dad. He knew he'd get a nice little lickin' if he wasn't right. Gene was a awful good boy. He still is a good boy. Never had a moment's trouble with him. He was that way ever since I can remember."

Mrs. Tenace recalled that Gene's dad began playing catch

with his son when Gene was two years old: "He be throwin' an official baseball at him. 'Now you catch this,' he'd say. Well, Gene couldn't *catch* the baseball. He was *two years old.* But his dad kept playin' with him at three and four years old.

"I remember one night when Gene was four and we lived in this apartment on Snyder Street in Philadelphia. Gene was at one end of the room, his father was at the other. One time Gene missed a baseball catch. The ball hit him in the mouth. Blood started drippin' down and tears did, too. His dad said, 'Don't cry or I'll give you a lickin'.' Gene didn't holler. I said to his dad, 'I'll take this ball and hit you in the head with it.'

"Gene respects his dad. I know he does, and he tells people he does. Gene's a man now, he's 26 and things are changing between him and his dad.

"During the play-offs Gene called the house from Detroit. He talked with his dad. I was in the other room so I didn't know what they was talking about. But his father was silent, save for a couple minutes. That's not like him. When he hung up he looked at me real funny. He said, 'Well, my son really hurt me. He said, "There you go criticizin' me again, dad."' Gene kinda stood up to his dad, I thought that was good.

"But I guess it all turned out for the best. Gene's ulcer is gone. He can eat anything he wants now. I think Gene is very happy with his life. He always wanted to be a major league baseball player. He's happy for himself, and I know he's pleased for his father, too.

"And his father! He's the most proudest person I've ever seen in my life. When we came back from the World Series in Cincinnati after Gene was named the best player by *Sport* magazine, you should have seen his father.

"I was driving the car 'cause his dad had a little too much champagne to drink. He sat in the back seat with our friends. He did all the talkin' for three hours, all the way home.

"He was saying how wonderful it was and he said, 'I got into the locker room to tell Gene I love him, and that he fulfilled all my dreams of bein' a major leaguer and bein' in the World Series.'

"Gene's dad was just in heaven. And he said, 'Ethel, did I tell you Gene said to tell mother I love her very much?'

"And I said, 'Yeah, you've told me about 20 times already.' "

Johnny Bench: Valedictorian and MVP

Tampa, March, 1972

Seven years ago, Johnny Bench gave the valedictory oration at his high school graduation ceremony. The speech was majestically entitled, "How the Youth of Today Will Be the Leaders of the Next Generation."

Speeches of this nature are often as forgettable as they are superficial. Bench's was no exception.

"I don't remember it myself," said Bench, the Cincinnati catcher, as he sat in the cool clubhouse. "I didn't even write it. A teacher did. Well, maybe I wrote a little of it. I was a naive 17-year-old kid growing up in Binger, Oklahoma, a town of 600. I had thoughts of grandeur then, but only about becoming a major league baseball player.

"Oh, there were some vague thoughts about making the world a better place to live. But I decided very early to back out on the presidency." Johnny Bench's roundish face broke into a smile; but quickly, his hazel eyes took on a serious, faraway look. His large right hand, a hand that can clutch seven baseballs at once, absently gripped most of his soft drink cup.

"It was a pretty depressing time in the country. John Kennedy had been assassinated less than two years before. And that was still with us. We were getting deeper and deeper into the Vietnam war. There was the bitterness of the race issue.

"I had set such lofty goals for myself, idealistic dreams, so high, so high." The dreams, however, were not about mankind, but about one man: Bench.

"Since I was four or five years old, that's all I wanted to be, a major league baseball player. I watched Mickey Mantle on television. He had been like me once, a kid from a small town in Oklahoma. I wanted to be a star like him, playing in all the great ball parks. And I wanted to have lots of money so that I could retire and go to Europe to ski, or go camping when I wanted, or play golf all over.

"And I think now that that's a good thing, to have a goal. For a time, young kids thought that they would drop out because they were down on society. But now I think they are returning to material things. Utopia without working for a living is nice, but impossible."

Bench left Binger immediately after high school to become a professional ball player. He signed with the Reds, and went to their Class A farm team in Tampa. He received only one bit of advice before going off into the real world. "Be careful of the women," said Bench senior.

"I had to grow up awful quick," Johnny Bench said. "There wasn't any room for boys. I had to learn for myself that there were phonies with get-rich-quick deals. I had to learn that there was no room for imperfection, that fans boo you. That is excruciating.

"I was lucky to meet Link Curtis in Tampa. He was a bonus player a few years before I signed. We hit it off right away. He saw that I was entering a world he had already entered. He looked after me. I didn't drink much. I never smoked. And I saw ballplayers around me doing those things. 'How could guys drink and smoke and still play ball?' I asked

Link. He explained the facts of life, like sometimes a little Scotch or beer can calm you down."

Johnny Bench came up to the majors late in 1967. He has been a star almost from the moment he first turned his red Cincinnati cap backwards. But after leading the Reds to a National League pennant in 1970, and being named the Most Valuable Player in the league, with 45 homers, 148 runs batted in and a .238 average, his education was broadening.

"Everybody wants a winner," said the 24-year-old Bench. "And when they don't get it, they're disappointed. They take it out on the player. They drive 150, 200 miles to a game, and then if you don't do what they expect—you strike out instead of hitting a homer—they boo. I don't go for that.

"Yeah, you become callous. You hear the boos and your stomach turns inside out. You try to drown out the boos in your mind. Try to block 'em out of your ears. You want to holler back at them. You'd like to see them boo you face-to-face. And they're the same people who later ask for your autograph.

"One game last year, my father was in the stands in Cincinnati. I struck out twice and popped up in my first three times at bat. Booing. Booing. Booing. My last time up. I got two strikes on me. Boo. Boo. Then I hit a home run to win the game. My dad jumped up and shouted, 'Boo now, you S.O.B.'s.' They didn't hear him. They were cheering.

"You have to have enough pride in yourself to keep pushing in those low times. A ballplayer is like an entertainer. I figure I'm serving a useful purpose if I can help people forget their troubles for a little while.

"Like at Christmastime, I go to hospitals. I see people dying of diseases that there are no cures for yet. I think, 'What can I do?' I talk to them, maybe make their day a bit brighter. I'd like to, I'd like to. But I still wonder if that's really enough. I've been the chairman of cancer drives and of a muscular dystrophy foundation in Cincinnati. I'm involved in the heart fund of the March of Dimes and in a children's fund.

"Bobby Kennedy said, 'I see things as they are and say why. I dream of things that never were and say why not.'

"In the end, I want my name to be known the way Stan Musial and Joe DiMaggio are known. They gained the respect of everybody. I want people to say I was a gentleman, too. I want people to say, 'Johnny Bench, he was a good man.' I hope I can make life a little more bearable for people."

Dan Gable: Just One Loss

Des Moines, Iowa, May, 1970

A magazine writer once described Dan Gable as "meek, quiet . . . who, like Clark Kent, peeks out at the world through horn-rimmed glasses" until he strips off his street clothes and "bounds onto the mat as—Superwrestler!"

In less high-flown words, Dan Gable is a sandy-haired, 5-foot-8½, 142-pound, 21-year-old Iowa State senior and two-time National Collegiate Athletic Association wrestling champion. He had won 181 straight matches through high school and college but, in the 1970 NCAA championship final—his last interscholastic match—he lost.

The next day, a three-inch thick Des Moines headline read: "Cyclones Win—But Gable Fails."

"I don't know what they mean by 'fail,' " said Gable. "I did the best I possibly could. I was out there. I never quit and I wrestled hard. But the loss has been hard for me to take. It was the biggest moment of my life.

"Afterward, people came over to me and said, 'You're still

the greatest.' My home town, Waterloo, was planning to give me a banquet and they said that now they want me more than ever. I don't know whether they're just saying that or whether it's true. I think it's true, though.

"Everybody feels sort of sorry for me. But it's better than them looking down on me. I've got a reputation for being a pretty straight guy. And they all know I've stayed in top shape. It's better than them saying that Dan Gable got what he deserved."

About 20 minutes after his close (13-11) loss to Larry Owings of Washington, Gable stood on the victory stand at Northwestern's McGraw Hall to receive his award for second place. He received a standing ovation from the capacity crowd of 8,500.

"It was hard to look up because I was crying and everything," recalled Gable. "And they just kept cheering. I realized inside that even though I got beat, I had to look up. And then they cheered twice as hard. Not that I was going berserk or anything, but, yeah, I kept crying.

"A lot of my friends said that it took a lot of courage to go out there. But I had to show up. Someone said something nice, that I had accepted defeat like I had accepted winning."

Myron Roderick, now the executive director of the United States Wrestling Federation, was a sensational college wrestler in the '50s who, like Gable, lost only one match. Roderick told Iowa State wrestling coach Harold Nichols, "I had a lot of wins, but that one loss made a man out of me."

"But he didn't lose his last match, in the national finals," said Gable. "It's too soon for me to know whether it made me more of a man. You know, I'm captain of our wrestling team. My perfect record made people look up to me, especially my teammates. Whatever I said they believed. I built up a lot of respect. And now? Well, a loss is a loss. I got whipped.

"I've never thought I was a Superman, even though I hadn't lost since I was 13, in junior high school. I am scared before every match. But I feel you have to excel in college, because in college you are setting yourself up for life. In high school, the important thing in sports is to participate. But in college, winning is the only thing."

Now, Gable's next objective is the 1972 U.S. Olympic team. "I'm the type of person who sets high goals and works hard to attain those goals—but I am only human."

He was asked if he likes being human.

"Nope," he said.

In 1972, Dan Gable won the Olympic lightweight wrestling gold medal.

Chris Evert: Rite of Passage

New York, October, 1974

It was inconceivable on that pleasant late summer afternoon in 1971 that this 16-year-old girl, her blond hair caught in a white ribbon, wearing a demure white dress on her slim frame, and walking with head modestly bowed as the 15,000 fans in the West Side tennis club applauded her entrance—it was inconceivable then that Chrissie Evert could ever be booed.

Three years later she was booed.

Chrissie Evert is no longer the sweetheart of America. She is a competitor, a corporation, a pro.

Three years ago, she came out of relative obscurity to reach the semifinals of the U.S. Open at Forest Hills. And when she emerged onto center court to play the Queen Bee, Billie Jean King, she was easily the sentimental favorite.

She was still the amateur, a high school junior. She had a peculiar two-handed backhand. She did not rush the net, but patiently stayed back at the baseline and allowed her opponent to make the mistake. "Just darling," was a phrase not infrequently heard about her.

Something else was demonstrated by Chrissie under those evenly overcast skies that September afternoon three years ago. Chrissie had a killer instinct. She lost to Billie Jean, but everyone knew she'd be back.

Much has changed for her, now that she is 19. She is engaged to the redoubtable Jimmy Connors, the Wimbledon and U.S. Open champion. He is a fervent competitor, too, but much more demonstrative. He shouts, spits, and flies into rages; sometimes he will even pull at his page boy haircut in anguish.

Chrissie, on the other hand, is brilliant in a mechanical way. She has in fact been labeled "The Ice Maiden."

Once, she declined $50,000 in prize money to maintain her amateur standing. Now, she has earned over $150,000 in winning 56 straight matches this year, up to the Forest Hills semifinals.

As a corporate entity, she receives a reported $100,000 a year from a manufacturer of tennis clothes. The manufacturer owns racehorses, one named after Chris. It's a championship horse, too.

Perhaps all this success has soured some fans, for when, in a rare moment, she grimaced with her thin-lipped face at a questionable call in the quarterfinals at Forest Hills, she was booed.

Chrissie, who is now called "Chris" or "Evert," said, stung, "I've noticed that in the last few weeks the crowd roots for the underdog."

Or they boo those with whom they have become disenchanted, those who have unwittingly sullied the stuff of which the fans' dreams have been fabricated.

Well, she isn't marrying a Prince Valiant with overflowing modesty; she isn't the darling pacific creature she appears to be; she isn't above accepting prize money and forsaking college to travel around the world as a tennis pro. She is turning into a woman, full of all the foibles—and glories—that make up a human being.

She is an athlete of the first order, to be sure. She demonstrated this above all question in her U.S. Open semifinal match this year against Evonne Goolagong, again at center court in Forest Hills. Chris had lost in the first set 6-0, and was losing in the second (of best of three) 4-3, Goolagong serving, when rain postponed the match.

It rained the next day. Now, on a sunny Sunday noon, the pair met again. With her careful, cool presence, Evert came back tenaciously to win the second set, 7-6.

In the third set, the fans began slowly to cheer her pluck. Evert the corporation, the betrayer of lame dreams, was deserving again of their admiration—if not their undying love, as in days of romantic yore.

In the shade of the marquee, Pancho Segura, the bronze-skinned, white-haired old tennis great, said, "Chris is such a tough competitor—you can tell because she is so patient." Goolagong was tough today, too. Four times she had Chris at match point, four times Evert wriggled out. "Evonne didn't lose those points," said Segura, "Chris won them."

Evert did not win the fifth match point, however.

Chris came off the court, her blond pony tail in a white ribbon, her white dress spotless, her tan legs smooth with the glint of sweat—and she was warmly applauded, just as she had been after losing to Billie Jean King in the semifinals three years ago.

But that was when she was a mere girl of 16, a hundred or so years ago.

Nate Ruffin: Survivor

Huntington, West Virginia, November, 1971

Nate Ruffin said he first heard about the crash when he walked out of a picture show in town on that misty, drizzling Saturday night and a girl he knew stopped him short.

"Her eyes were big like this," said Nate, "and she said, 'How'd you make it?'

" 'Make what?' I asked. She looked at me like I was something dead. Then she fainted."

Nate Ruffin, co-captain and defensive back for the Marshall University football team, had not made the trip to Greenville, North Carolina, to play East Carolina State on November 14, 1970. He would soon undergo an operation for calcium deposits on his right bicep. Nate's seat was taken by a member of The Big Green, the school alumni-and-friends booster club.

So Nate, by the haphazards of fate, was not on the plane that carried home that Big Green member and other local team supporters, including shopkeepers, legislators, doctors, lawyers, dentists, and 34 of Nate's teammates, plus the entire football coaching staff, the athletic director, the sports information director, and some of their wives. Seventy-five in all.

Nate was not on the Southern Airways DC-9 that rainy night when the plane, flying for the mountaintop Tri-State Airport, hit the tops of pine trees instead, cartwheeled into a mountainside and disintegrated. Teams of scientists were sent down from Washington, D.C., and after two weeks of laborious work, 69 bodies were positively identified. The remains of six others, all players were buried in a common grave.

It was the worst American sports team disaster in history, and followed by a month the crash that killed 14 Wichita State football players and their coaches.

Nate Ruffin, one year later, can talk about the crash calmly. No hint of tears in Nate's brown eyes, as he sits on a dormitory couch. His black face is gentle, absorbed, intelligent, without facade. His voice is slightly husky. His body, 6 feet, 180 pounds, though solid, seems slight.

"I said I'd never play any more ball," said Nate Ruffin. "I felt no desire. All my friends were gone. I figured I didn't have to play anyway. I've got these calcium deposits and the doctors say that if I get a blow a certain way on the nerve, my right arm will become paralyzed for life. You know, I couldn't unbend my arm for six months. I learned to do everything left-handed."

After awhile, Nate changed his mind about playing. "I wanted to be a part of this young team, this rebuilding team," he said. "I guess I felt an obligation to the dead, too."

Nate is a senior, the last living link of a Marshall team that had the school's first undefeated freshman squad, in 1968; then suffered through the disillusionment and embarrassment of a recruiting scandal that resulted in Marshall being indefinitely suspended from the Mid-American Conference in 1969; then underwent a thorough housecleaning—a team that had hopes of becoming one of the best in Marshall history.

"The greatest memory of that team," said Nate, "was when we beat Bowling Green in 1969. If we lost to them, we would have broken the national record for winless games at 28. The whole week was called, 'Stop the Streak Week' on campus. Oh, we were so fired up for that game. BG was a powerhouse, a big favorite. We won 27-16. The Green Bay Packers couldn't have beat us that Saturday."

Nate was one of three starters who did not make the trip to East Carolina State. The other two were Ed Carter and Felix Jordan. Jordan, like Nate, had been injured. Carter's case was eerie. His father had died a few days before and Carter, of course, attended the funeral. His mother asked Ed to stay home with her for that weekend.

Carter and Jordan are juniors now. They and Nate formed the nucleus of the new team, a team seemingly a kind of crazy quilt, with a few transfer students, some walk-ons, green kids off last year's frosh team, and greener kids who last season were playing for high schools in Barrackville, W. Va.; Toronto, Ohio; Louisa, Ky.; Pleuna, Ala.

Twenty of the 22 starters are freshmen and sophomores. The team is playing the same schedule, against the same tough, experienced opponents that the crash victims would have played. In its first home game this season, Marshall was a 20-point underdog against Xavier, and won on a last-second touchdown. It was called, around town, "the miracle game." Marshall lost its next game to Miami (Ohio), 66-6, and lost the two after that. But on Homecoming against Bowling Green, a team with bowl aspirations, a team that had beaten Miami by 30 points, Marshall dominated the game and won.

"It seemed like these were more than just football games, just like the season seems like more than just a football season," said Marshall's new football coach, Jack Lengyel. "We're a kind of symbol, I think. It may sound corny, but I think we're symbolizing the spirit of America, the idea of proving that you can come back from adversity."

Charlie Nash: Toughest Olympian

Munich, September, 1972

Charlie Nash slept like a baby through the burst of gunfire in the night between the guerrilla Arabs and the German police. "Made me feel at home," he said. He in fact had trouble sleeping when he first got to the Olympic Village because it was so tranquil.

Nash, the Irish lightweight boxing champion, is from the Creggan Estate in Derry, Northern Ireland, an occupied, bloody battleground between the Irish Republican Army and the British Army.

"The bombs and the shootin' goin' off at home put me to sleep now," he says. "They used to keep me starin' at the ceilin'. Now if I don't hear a whale of a lot of shootin' I stay awake. I think maybe there's somethin' really terrible just around the corner."

Nash may be the toughest kid at the Olympics. He had dodged bombs and bullets and officious British soldiers to get to his gym to train for the Games. And yet he nearly had to be withdrawn from the boxing competition because of a busted-up pinky.

When he finally landed in the Munich ring, it was the harmless hard head of a Dane that almost did him in. Nash, a 5-foot-7, 132-pound southpaw counterpuncher, beat Erik Madsen of Denmark in the opening round of lightweight boxing. He won with hardly his thick brown mustache getting sweaty. Only his bobbing cowlick seemed to get a workout. But Nash hurt the little finger of his hand when, in the first round, "I give him a wee bit of a hammer."

The hand swelled. He was rushed off for X rays. "His hand's gone," whispered one of the ashen retinue of boxing teammates hurrying along to the hospital.

Nash's blue eyes were expressionless. "Imagine goin' through all I gone through and maybe bein' put out because of a pinky? Well, worse things can happen."

Like what happened to Willie Nash, 19, Charlie's younger brother by two years. He was shot and killed while marching in the peaceful civil demonstration on infamous Bloody Sunday last February about a half-mile down the bogside from the Nash home.

"Me father was shot as well, but he was only wounded," said Charlie. "I cannot understand the shootin' by the British soldiers that day. My brother was still wearin' the black suit from the night before when our other brother was married."

Training for the Olympic dream was a literal nightmare for Charlie, starting with sleeping.

He could not do roadwork when he returned home evenings from his job as a guillotine operator in a printing factory. "I didn't dare run on the road for fear of gettin' shot," he said. "There are lots of British foot soldiers aboot. Some of 'em are a wee nervous. Well, what would you do if you saw a boy shootin' past?"

Getting to his club, St. Mary's, only about 300 yards from his home, was a rugged affair. He has been stopped as many as six times on the way to the gym. "I reckon I look suspicious carryin' me duffel bag," he said. "They ask me, 'What's up, boy?' Then they empty out alla me trainin' gear."

To save time Charlie began to take back roads. He would leave his home on Dunree Gardens Street, slip down Melmore Gardens, go up Leenon Gardens, around to Malan Gardens, over to Dunmore Gardens and finally make it to the end of Innissown Gardens where the club is, dodging into the shadow of a building when soldiers clicked by.

He says he couldn't relax even when he got to the gym because of the bombings and the bomb threats. But then he'd do his daily total of 20 rounds of sparring, bag punching, rope skipping, and medicine ball (four rounds each). He did 20 rounds instead of the customary 12 to make up for his lack of roadwork.

"But sometimes," he said, "I would just stick in the house and do me exercises when there was too much of the shootin' outside."

For the first time in history, Northern Ireland athletes could be part of Ireland's Olympic team instead of the Great Britain team. Some of Nash's countrymen, like pentathlon winner Mary Peters, were asked to participate with the British and did. Not Nash. "I don't think it's right for foreigners to rule our country," he said.

He had trouble concentrating on his training during the Olympics because he worried about home. "There are only British newspapers in the Olympic Village," he said, "and they only tell what they want you to hear."

He can't turn professional because that would mean leaving Northern Ireland. (There is no pro fighting there). "I don't want to walk away from the troubles at home," he said.

X rays of Charlie's hand proved negative. But the hand remained swollen when he next knocked out a Spaniard in 40 seconds of the first round. In the quarterfinals, he lost to a wily, 33-year-old Pole who had cunningly butted him. Nash then openly butted the Pole in return. The referee disqualified Nash.

Charlie Nash was not crushed. "This is just child's play compared to back home," he said. "But I am retirin'. I am thinkin' it is aboot time I get married and settle down. Fightin's no kinda life."

Dave Cowens: Reluctant Paul Bunyan

March, 1973

The directions to Dave Cowens' house read like the directions Columbus might have jotted for himself on his first voyage across uncharted seas: Try here, try there, a little this way, a little that, and bingo!, the new world.

Come off the Mass Pike into Weston, about 20 miles west of Boston, says Cowens, then you go under a railroad trestle and around a curve and onto a blacktop road and you'll run into a wooden fence and a dirt driveway and some fir trees and that's where I live, in the beach house. The address is 164 Orchard Avenue. Well, not quite.

His rented house has no address. The house on the hill of a 4½-acre estate has the address. On top of that, the closest beach is 20-some miles away. Cowens lives way down the hill alongside a large empty pool. The investment made for all this explorational information was a long wandering through the woods and a $20 cab fare.

The cab eventually sniffed out the place and the passenger disembarked at the foot of the driveway ("I'm not driving up there," said the cabbie, asserting that the steep rutted and rocky driveway with an unwashed maroon Chevy at the top was the final straw).

The 6-foot-9 Cowens emerged on the porch of the one-room cabana house to greet the visitor. Cowens was wearing a green plaid woolen shirt, brown corduory pants held up by suspenders, and tan Hush Puppy shoes. He looked like Norman Rockwell's idea of a basketball player: a cross between Huck Finn and Paul Bunyan.

In the house, Cowens pulled up a folding chair for himself and invited the visitor to sit on the yellow convertible couch. The only other chair in the house is a platform rocker which Cowens proudly says he bought for only $25 in a Maine antique shop.

Sitting there, Cowens gave a tour of the house. He pointed to one corner. "That's my living room," he said, "and over there is my dining room and here is my den and over there is my office and you're sitting on my bedroom."

To dispel any ideas that these digs are not sumptuous, Cowens adds that "I've also got a kitchen, a bathroom and"—the pièce de résistance—"a pretty big closet."

Why would the 25-year-old center for the Boston Celtics, the man recently named the 1973 Most Valuable Player in the National Basketball Association, a public figure who must command a hefty salary, why would he be simulating a 20th century Thoreau? (Thoreau's Walden Pond, incidentally, is only a few miles from Cowens's Weston).

"For one thing," he said, "you can be free out here. I mean, if I want to run outside and holler and scream and go crazy, I can. I haven't yet, but the option is always open.

"I don't like the city and apartment house living. You're like an automaton. You press the elevator button to take you up to your apartment, which looks like everyone else's apartment. You have your designated parking space. And the traffic! As soon as the light turns green the car behind you honks like a conditioned response."

He also feels that life away from the city gives him time to leisurely and pleasurably look at his life, where it is and where it is going.

"Sometimes friends visit me. And I take walks through the woods, or I walk about a mile and a half into town or I go fishing at my pond, which is filled with bass, pickerel—every time you cast you catch something," said Cowens, who wouldn't divulge the pond's location.

"It gives you a perspective, being out here. You think about being idolized because you are a basketball player. It's absurd. A basketball player is nothing important. He really doesn't contribute to making people's lives happier. Not like a plumber or a fireman, or even a businessman."

As an entertainer, it was suggested, doesn't a basketball player create joy for spectators?

"I'm sure a plumber gives people enjoyment."

Then why does he play basketball?

"It's one of the things I do best," he said. "I like the competition and I like the responsibility of being part of a team. It's like a job that I enjoy. And I make good money. That's important—for the future. So I invest in something.

"There are immediate rewards for me in basketball. I work to get open for a basket, throw a fake, and score. There are also immediate failures. You know, I miss the basket. You strive to be consistent. That's reality. What is very important for me is that in basketball I am always taking a positive action. I am confident and going toward something definite, a definite goal.

"That's probably why people say I'm a fierce basketball player. Off the court, I'm actually passive. I'm insecure in a way. Like with business dealing, I get some offers and I'm really not sure how to handle them. I spend time at my desk there going over these offers. Luckily I've got a good lawyer-business manager who works with me and who is helping me learn about these things.

"But I'm still searching for what I want to do when I'm through with basketball. I'm fortunate in that I haven't been thrust immediately into the work force. I can piddle around and think about my future.

"I'm conservative until I'm positive, then I'm the other way around.

"Right now, I'm thinking about the land and the farm I'm building for my family—my parents and four brothers and sister, who live in Newport, Kentucky. We're going to raise some pigs and chickens and some crops. Maybe I'll be a farmer.

"I majored in criminology at Florida State. I might get into that field in some way. I also took courses in mechanics and I've thought about owning a service station. I'd be a general mechanic. You always need those fellas.

"If I stay in basketball, it would probably be as a high school coach. I wouldn't want to go higher. I wouldn't want to get involved in the politics and pressures of it, the recruiting. I'd want the boys to come out and I'd take what I got and I'd try to mold them into a team."

Cowens himself was a standout at Newport Catholic High and Florida State University, though no All-American. He was chosen in the first round of the draft by the Celtics. He joined the team when Bill Russell retired. Cowens, at first thought too small to be a pro center, eventually won the position by his hustle and quickness. He is now averaging about 20 points and 16 rebounds a game and led the Celtics as they won more games than any other team in the NBA.

"Because you're in the public eye, people are always gushing over you, telling you how great you are, and all that mushy malarkey.

"They want my autograph. *My* autograph. For what? Maybe I'm a jerk. Maybe I'm a heel. How do they know?

"They just see me play basketball. They want you to be what they want to be. So I have to keep remembering what I really am. I'm the guy who loses his temper in a bar fracas. I'm the guy who in high school told my parents that I was sleeping at a friend's house and then drove around all night in a car, drinking beer. But I'm also the guy who tries to do people favors, treat them as human beings—the way I'd like to be treated—and who is trying to mature, trying to learn as I grow older."

Days here go quickly for Cowens (who pays $185 a month rent from September through May). Right now he is involved in reading about architecture, since he will contribute ideas to the building of his parents' farm house. He'll put on the wall stereo and listen to semiclassical music. Or light a fire in the fireplace.

Then he may cook himself a meal. He says he usually makes soup or a large ham or a casserole, something that lasts long.

While he's cooking, he may intermittently shoot a Nerf ball at the little basket hanging on the kitchen door, and, on the day of a game, he'll get dressed—a euphemism—by hanging a tie on whatever outfit he happens to be wearing. Red Auerbach, Celtic general manager, wants all his players to wear a tie to the game. "Does this striped tie go with the striped shirt? I'm really not big on clothes," Cowens admits, unnecessarily.

His favorite pregame meal these days is a tuna noodle casserole. His "recipe" is not very special, he confesses. "You can get it off of any Mueller's noodle box," he said. But it's so good, he adds, that he once ate three large portions at one sitting. And got sick.

Cowens insists, though, that he is no gourmet cook. Recently, for example, he wanted to make something special for himself for breakfast. So he called his mother in Kentucky for advice.

"Mom," he asked, "how do you make soft-boiled eggs?"

Cookie Wallace: Up 'n' Comer

Tampa, March, 1970

It was the fourth time he had been knocked down. This time Cookie Wallace flumped and made a hammock of the bottom ring rope. His scuffed and deeply scarred white boxing shoes lay still. The referee did not bother to count, but waved his arms to signal the fight in the sixth round was finished. He then raised Bob Foster's long arm in triumph.

It was a non-title fight, and the purpose was simply to keep Foster, the light heavyweight champion, in trim and in pin money until his next title defense, and after that a hopeful shot at Joe Frazier and the heavyweight title.

In this seedy Tampa, Florida, armory, the crowd of some 2,500—those seated on unsure folding chairs at ringside, those in the two paint-peeling balconies—cheered for the winner who did what they all knew he would, or grumbled for the underdog who, as he would say later, "got up from three knockdowns by the champ. Not many men can say that."

The fans watched and shouted as Wallace finally rose and walked across the ring to congratulate Foster. Then there was a sharp gasp from the crowd as Wallace's knees buckled and he collapsed again.

A doctor was at his side now, and Wallace's handler sponged his neck, and Cookie was up, smiling with crooked teeth within a scraggly patch of mustache and goatee. But

Cookie's muscular brown torso was still not quite sure of the direction his thick legs would wobble.

Wallace is 22 years old, has a wife and four children, and works on a cargo ramp for Braniff Airlines in Dallas. He has been fighting for three years, and thinks he's had some 45 bouts, and believes he has won more than he has lost. He recently dumped his manager who, he said, was stickin' it to him and now he manages himself and it is not so easy gettin' good fights.

"I was takin' this fight for the buck," he would say later. "I need a little cash right quick. I got liability with the car, and that sort of thing."

Now, Foster sat in the corner of a little dark room and his left hand was in an ice bucket. He assured the small group of reporters that his hand was all right, he just wasn't taking any chances on injury.

The questions concerned Frazier, and of course Foster said he could beat him and, with a wry smile under his thin mustache, he said don't nobody tell Frazier about that right hook they saw tonight because it's a secret weapon and Frazier thinks Foster only got a left jab. No one asked about Wallace.

Soon, however, Wallace appeared quietly, smiling broadly. ("I'm the type of fighter, I like everybody and I want for everybody to like me," he says). He wore a black leather car coat, with the hem loose, and the cuffs of his blue jeans were rolled up. Wallace apologized to Foster for what Foster complained in the ring was butting.

"I didn't try to fight dirty," Wallace told him. "I was just tryin' to get inside." He hunched his shoulders and shadowboxed a bit.

"I know that," said Foster, kindly. "But that's the way champs do. You want the other guy to think he's fighting dirty."

They shook hands and Wallace departed. Now Foster began a little story of when Yank Durham, Frazier's manager, came by recently and newspaper photographers shot Foster hitting the big bag with Durham holding it.

"Whop, whop, whop," said Foster, his lean left hand out of the bucket and whiplashing the air. "My manager, Billy Edwards here, he said, 'Goddam, you don't have to hit the bag so hard. We'll never get a shot at Frazier.' "

At the box office, waiting for his 20 per cent of the gate, "He hit me so hard and so fast" Wallace said, "that I didn't realize I was hit until I tried to move my legs. Then I sank. It was like putting a gas mask on when you get ready for an operation. You just get weaker all of a sudden.

"I knew nobody gave me a chance tonight. But I felt if I could get inside him, keep a-movin', keep a-pushin' until I get my right cross, then I could knock him out.

"But he don't trade punches. No, he's a jolly good fellow. Takes his time, bam, bam, bam. But at least people can say that Cookie fought Bobby Foster, the champ. I think it'll help me get some more fights. They'll say I'm someone who's comin' up."

Afterward, Cookie Wallace became Foster's sparring partner, and helped him prepare for the Frazier fight. Frazier knocked Foster out in two rounds.

Basketball as Drama: "The Ruckers"

August, 1972

"Basketball is a form of dramatic art. And in places like Harlem, basketball may be the only great drama the people ever get to see and feel and enjoy."—Bobby Hunter of the Harlem Globetrotters in The City Game.

Hard to tell where exactly that bright shout sprang from. Maybe from one of those kids hunched in one of those trees around this Harlem schoolyard basketball court. Maybe from one of those young dudes with a floppy applejack cap and soul-music radio who crowded into the hot bleachers.

It was certainly too close and too clear to have come from one of those folks hanging out of curtain-still windows in the project buildings across Eighth Avenue. Or from someone waiting for the CC Local on the elevated train platform, fanning himself with a newspaper on this miserably hot Sunday afternoon. And it was too squeaky to have come from any of the middle-aged men or matrons seated around the court on beach chairs and milk crates.

"Let 'em go into overtime," the caller implored. Some fans laughed, others clapped. The game, nearly over, was a runaway, something like 130-100. But it was magnificent stuff. Especially a guy named Frank Streety, nicknamed "Shake 'n' Bake," who is a dribbler for the Harlem Globetrotters.

Streety was performing a high and wonderful kind of theater. The fans wanted not so much more of the game, but much more of Streety. This was the Rucker Tournament, which, like true art, is concerned more with style than score. So Streety is an unmitigated hit.

He has more quick stops and jerks than any of the chrome-dazzled cars that pull up to the high, wire-fenced park, more twists than the pretzel vendors, and more cool than the snow-cone sellers who hawk in a motley row as the thousand-plus people enter the park for the great Harlem theater event of the week.

Much of the drama is provided by the big names, national figures such as Wilt Chamberlain (who will still drop in for a game or two a season) and Connie Hawkins and Bill Bradley and Julius Irving (who commutes from Atlanta) and Bob Love (who commutes from the Midwest)—they play without pay in what must be the best summer league in the country.

These heralded players go against the local stars, such as Helicopter Knowings and Earl Manigault. "Reps" are on the line. "Your game is O.K. for downtown," one fan shouts at former Knick Nate Bowman when a ball is stolen, "but not for uptown."

The tournament was begun in 1952 by a neighborhood schoolteacher named Holcomb Rucker, who died a few years ago of cancer at age 38, and is now discussed in reverential tones. There are now 11 teams playing on summer weekends, and they have such sponsors as Vitalis, No-Tox plastic model glue, Nerf balls, the Urban League and Small's Paradise (a Harlem night club once owned by Wilt). The Ruckers was initially begun as a program to keep boys off the streets. It has worked to a considerable degree.

Yet it is common that for every star spawned in these ghetto schoolyards who escapes to big-time college ball or the pros, there are 20 others from the same block who go to drugs or the morgue.

A husky player named Green now caught the crowd's fancy in the second game. He banged in a rebound for two points. "That's the monster play!" said Walt Simpson, who provides a witty, wise play-by-play on a public address system. Shortly after, an overly inspired Green blew a stuff shot. The ball clanked against the back rim and bounded up and away, while Green fell heavily to the asphalt. "The basket monstered him back!" said Simpson. The crowd laughed. So, eventually, did Green.

Legends have naturally developed over the years of great plays, great one-on-one confrontations. And the involved crowd, like the tattered penny gallery of Shakespeare's Globe Theater, urges the participants on. "Fly, 'Copter, Fly," they'll yell. And "Dance, Earl, Dance."

That last plea came in the third and final game of the day. Earl Manigault is one of the local legends. He grew up here, had monumental potential. For reasons only he might know, he turned to drugs. He touched the nation when his story—

his downfall and then triumph over drugs—was told in *The City Game,* Pete Axthelm's fine book on New York City basketball. Manigault was given a tryout by a reader, Utah Stars owner Bill Daniels. But Earl's reflexes had been considerably sapped. He didn't make the team.

Earl is 6 foot 2, slim, can still jump like 6 foot 8. Sleepy and with an inscrutable, rather toothless smile, he looks at first unimposing. And then! He took a rebound in what they call here "Death Alley"—the middle lane—and soared, *soared* straight up and with his back to the basket laid the ball softly up for two. The crowd leaped instantly. It was an absolutely electric moment, so swift, so graceful, so unexpected.

The sun was sinking behind the projects now, casting long shadows of the players on the court. There were final appeals by Simpson to community spirit to sign a petition for a Harlem sports arena. There was mention of the Harlem Professionals, Inc., a group that works to get college scholarships for ghetto kids.

It was over now, Shake 'n' Bake's shakin' 'n' bakin', the Monster Man's dunk manqué, Manigault's shot, the stylishness of Elnardo Webster of the Memphis Pros, each adding his piece to the mosaic legend, art, communal theater of Harlem, of the Ruckers, of basketball. Fans and players now return to the streets of Harlem where, as in an overwritten novel, men and women sit on hot stoops in the night, where rats and roaches and children share the same bed, where some despairing young men and women murder themselves with needles in peeling hallways. Who will survive?

The drama of the court ends. The drama of the streets is endless.

Prime Time

There is a confidence and courage that comes with achievement. And the athlete in his heyday feels a fullness in mind and body that may never be equalled—though he may not know it, or consider it.

Kathy Switzer and the Knife

New York, October, 1974

The sun's morning rays were already growing warm as they spilled in an orange stream across the East River, and then onto the concrete promenade where Kathy Switzer ran. A boat horn sounded; birds were in the trees. She felt easy and light. It was a beautiful morning. And when she heard the footsteps behind her she turned and looked, more out of instinctive curiosity than alarm.

A hundred or so yards behind, she saw a man in sweatshirt and sweat pants in a leisurely trot—obviously a fellow jogger. Subconsciously she felt relieved about that.

Kathy has had some uncomfortable experiences while jogging alone. Now, she always clips a pencil-thin aerosol can of "dog spray" to the drawstring of her sweat pants, to ward off some dogs and some people.

One afternoon several months ago, while jogging through Central Park, five tough-looking youths jumped out of the bushes. As Kathy came up hill in her 18th mile, the boys made lip-smacking sounds and said how they liked her long legs and supple body. She recalls now that she was too tired even to be scared, paid them no heed, jogged around them and continued down the hill. They were too stunned by her insouciance to follow.

When she runs on the promenade, she runs along the iron barrier beside the river, as opposed to running close to the park area. It is similar to the precaution of the gunfighter who always sits in a saloon with his back to the wall.

The footsteps were coming closer behind her. She did not turn around this time. Just another case of fragile male ego, she said to herself. Men often pass her, she believes, because they don't like the feeling of running behind a woman.

Anyway, she did not want to think further about those footsteps. Kathy was in training for an important race for her, the Olympic Airways-sponsored New York City marathon run of 26 miles, 385 yards. In the last year she has made tremendous progress in her times. She says she has cut 20 minutes off her time. With blue eyes smiling, she adds that she has lost 20 pounds, too.

This marathon event is important because she hopes to run it in less than three hours, a feat she equates to a miler breaking the four-minute barrier. And the satisfaction of such improvement over the year has been euphoric, she says. "The feeling—that you are doing all you can to be the best you can—is incredible," she has said.

Kathy received national attention when she became the first female to run in the Boston Marathon, in 1967, when she was a 19-year-old college student at Syracuse University. She had signed the application form "K. V. Switzer" and wore a hooded sweatshirt on this rainy day. She was finally discovered when the day brightened and she removed her excess clothing while running. The Marathon's co-director, Jock Semple, a white-haired Scotsman, believing she was desecrating the event, gave her hell with his brogue and tried to rip the number off her back. Fellow runners came to her aid, and she remained in the race to the finish.

Later, the Amateur Athletic Union barred her and other women from competing with men (she had run distance on her college team, too). She successfully fought that ruling, with the help of others. In 1972 she was running in the Boston Marathon again, but this time legally.

Kathy Switzer has been striving since the Boston Marathon of 1967 to earn a place for herself and other women athletes in the male-dominated sports world. She feels women, even in athletic events, are always looked at as women first and athletes last, by officials, some participants, and many spectators. She recalls in her first Boston Marathon when, after some 20 miles, she was so fatigued she could hardly keep her eyes open. Strangely, she heard clapping. She opened her eyes and saw an elderly couple alongside the road, and the lady was applauding.

Kathy figured the lady was cheering her perseverance. As Kathy jogged by, she held her head high and overheard the lady say, "Look dearie, isn't that cute—it's a girl and she's wearing earrings!"

The the slapping steps behind her got closer, louder. A sudden wash of panic came over Kathy. The man shot his arm around her neck. He stuck a steak knife under her ear. Kathy couldn't scream; the sound was caught in the pit of her stomach.

"Gimme your money," he said. "I'm gonna cut you."

He was about 5 foot 8, an inch or so taller than she. He weighed about 160 pounds, some 35 pounds more than Kathy. His arm around her neck was viselike.

She heard her voice, coming from some distant place, saying, so absurdly rational in this monstrous moment, "But you can plainly see I have no money."

"Come with me," he said. He began pulling her toward the cluster of trees and bushes. "I'm gonna cut you."

Sights and sounds and thoughts swirled for Kathy. The trees, the sun, the concrete, the smell of the man, the pressure of his muscles, the squashing of her neck, the sparkle of the river, the knife point jabbing the flesh behind her ear. Thoughts of rape, of no help nearby, of being slashed, and, how crazy it seemed later in the telling, the rage at how unfair that all her vigorous training for the marathon should be washed away in a pool of her own blood.

She knew she had to get her hand on that aerosal can

clipped to her sweat pants, and hidden under her warmup jacket.

The man wasn't aware of Kathy's attempt to get the can. She knew even under this great pressure that she could not make a mistake, had to be precise, couldn't drop the can, had to get the hole pointed in the exact direction.

She touched the can. And now everything went fantastically slow, like in a dream sequence. She brought the can up, spraying all the way. She remembers seeing the stream of spray—the sun filtering through it—rising from the man's waist to his chest to his neck to his chin and into his eyes.

The man clutched his eyes and ran blindly off. Kathy dashed in the opposite direction. She got to a phone and called her friend Phillip at their apartment. He called the police.

Kathy, shaken, soon pulled herself together and a couple of hours later was in her office, working at her public relations job at AMF, a sports equipment company.

And after work, before dark, she jogged her regular evening route of 10 miles. Kathy Switzer still had a marathon to run.

Pete Rose and Ty Cobb

"A Pete Rose by any other name still stinks," scribbled one neo-Shakespearean paraphrast on a banner in October of 1973 in Shea Stadium.

This literary brainstorm was conceived after Pete Rose of the Cincinnati Reds slammed into Bud Harrelson of the Mets while trying to break up a double play. Dust, spikes, and a fist or two flew.

When Rose returned to his left-field position, after the

nefarious inning, boos and whizzing beer bottles greeted him.

Nothing new for Rose. Bleacher bums in Wrigley Field pelt him with paper clips. Fans in San Francisco bathe him with invective. Even hometown Cincinnati fans, as well as some players, figuratively hold their nose when they hear the name Rose.

He is called hot dog for his headfirst slides, his rifling the ball into the infield after a meaningless out, his executioner-like motion after catching a fly ball, his running, running even on walks. He has been called, not always with admiration, "Charley Hustle."

"Well," says Rose, "nobody liked Ty Cobb either."

Rose sees himself in the mold of a modern-day Ty Cobb. Rose is a man who hits for average. In 1973 he batted .338, to win his third league hitting title in his ninth straight season hitting over .300.

The similarities between Rose and Cobb are interesting, both in playing skills and attitude, but the differences are even more absorbing. They differ mainly in degree.

Cobb had a lifetime batting average of .367 for 24 seasons. Rose, going into his 12th big-league year, has a .312 career average.

"Cobb was a super hitter," said Lew Fonseca, the American League batting champion in 1929 and currently a sometime hitting coach with the Cincinnati Reds, "and Pete is a fine hitter.

"I think overall Cobb was more talented, but both showed tremendous desire and used their skills to the ultimate.

"Pete is always asking me about Cobb. I remember his first question. 'Tell me, Lew, was Cobb as tough as they say?'

" 'Tougher,' I told him."

Cobb was always getting in brawls, with teammates, with opponents and with fans, who he would climb into the stands to wound.

"Cobb would do anything to win," said Fonseca. "I remember a story concerning Howard Ehmke, the pitcher. He had pitched at Detroit when Cobb was the playing-manager. Then he was traded to Philadelphia. The first game Ehmke was in against Detroit, Ehmke hit Cobb with a pitch. And Ehmke called to Cobb, 'I hit 20 batters for you last year. Now I got one for myself.' "

Cobb would snarl at the opposition, said Fonseca. And, in his way, so does Rose. "One pitcher got Pete out three straight times," said Fonseca. "The fourth time up, Pete shouted to him, 'Go down to the bullpen and get warmed up, you ain't got nothin.' "

One major difference is that Cobb often did not even speak to teammates. Rose talks, though sometimes double-edged. When Rose says to Tony Perez, who passes him in the locker room, "When you gonna knock me in? I'm tired of standin' on second base," it draws a laugh from Perez. And a slow smile from Rose.

Cobb, particularly, was obsessed with being tops. Once, he was angered when he returned to his hotel room saw his roommate in the bathtub. Cobb screamed, "Get out of there —I'm always first!"

Rose has his peculiarities, too. Once he was giving a baseball clinic for kids on a Hamilton, Ohio, sandlot field, and he let a grounder go through his legs. One kid laughed. Rose skewered him with a look and said, "I make seven errors a season. I have six left."

Both Rose and Cobb were influenced by their fathers. Rose's father taught him to switch-hit ("And I'll always do it, I promised Dad that")—and emphasized to young Pete how Enos Slaughter always hustled everywhere on the field.

He told Pete, "That stuff about it's not whether you win or lose, but how you play the game, that's a lot of bunk. If you don't win, you haven't accomplished anything."

"If my father were alive," said Rose, "he'd have bawled me out if I hadn't put the slug on Harrelson."

In his autobiography, written with Al Stump, Cobb talks about the tragedy of his father's death. "My father had his head blown off with a shotgun when I was 18 years old . . . I've never gotten over it."

It seems that Cobb tried ever after to vindicate his father and produced, in Stump's words, "the most violent, successful, thoroughly maladjusted personality ever to pass across American sports."

As Cobb himself put it, "I had to fight all my life to survive. They were all against me . . . but I beat the bastards and left them in the ditch."

Tom Seaver: Summertime Achilles

New York, April, 1972

Tom Seaver believed that the baseball players' strike, in the end, would have little effect on the fan. As the clouds gather around the double play at second base and the heat of the pennant race warms in August, the fan would forget the passions of the recently-ended spring strike. The fan often has a memory fuse as short as his temper. "What have you done for us lately?" is all he asks, all he's ever asked.

"The only thing that will be relevant to the fan," said Tom Seaver, the Mets' star pitcher and player representative, "is how his team is doing and how the individual players are making out."

For now, though, there seems to be a souring. The fan stares into his glass of beer and bemoans his knickered heroes. He still cannot accept the realism that they are actually mortal men who play this kid's game, and play it for profit. They play it, not only because—like that fan—they love it, but also to provide a security for their families and a livelihood today.

Yet heroes are expected to be cut from a wholly different cloth. They may look like the rest of us, but they must act and perform like demigods.

"Baseball heroes," wrote Tristram Coffin, in *The Old Ball Game,* "strutting and fretting upon an artificial stage, find their personalities being crammed into basic stereotypes that the world seems never to have been without." So Willie Mays and Tom Seaver are contemporary America's summertime version of Hercules and Achilles.

Of course, our psyche permits us not to look upon these mortal men as mercenaries. We give little thought to the fact that a man from Hackensack and another from Caracas play for the Chicago Cubs, and a man from Punxsutawney, Pa., and another from Muskegon are with Baltimore.

And so we are shocked and benumbed by such mundane matters as money—for them. And besides, what money! We hear of $100,000-a-year salaries, $200,000-a-year salaries. And we feel an encrouching cynicism: Are these romantic heroes Hessians?

No, they are simple men, trained in the ways of a capitalistic society. The system tells us that we can earn as much as our expertness and as much as the laws of supply and demand dictate. Yet under the reserve clause (in which an owner determines a player's baseball life) and under the monopolistic power (that makes contract "haggling" a ritual and nothing more), the professional baseball player lives outside the system.

The point is not that players often make a great deal of money in comparison to your local butcher but that they aren't accorded all they might earn in a free market. For example, major league clubs' gate receipts have increased to 80 times what they were in 1883 but the average players' salary has increased only seven times in the same period (according to Dr. Harold Seymour, author of *Baseball: The Golden Age*).

"And," said Tom Seaver, "not all of the players make over $100,000 a year. Many make $20,000 and less. And they have great expenses—like living in three different places: a spring training home, their club's hometown and their off-season home.

"Yet the players' strike had more to do with ethics and reason than just money matters. We feel we've been taken advantage of by the owners. When Charley Finley can tell Vida Blue that he has to sign for what Finley wants him to, or not play at all, well, that's grossly unfair.

"It's true," said Seaver, "that we get up in the morning and look forward to going to work. A steelworker probably doesn't. But our job is not all that easy. Follow me around in the hot days of August."

Seaver mirrors something Ed Walsh, a long-ago great pitcher, said. Walsh once worked in coal fields. "This being regarded as a star pitcher is a harder job than being a coal miner," he said.

There have been a handful of strikes and threatened strikes in baseball history, dating all the way back to 1890. The owners even then termed the players "ingrates" and "anarchists." The faithful fans were appalled at the players' rapacity. (Even so divine a hero as Walter Johnson was, during a contract dispute, vilified in his headline: "Almighty Dollar Johnson's Ideal.")

However, the fans still came. It is not so easy to live a humdrum life and have no hero to cheer, no bum to boo.

Frenchy Fuqua, or Count Peacock

Pittsburgh, December, 1972

Frenchy Fuqua's terrible wrath was visited upon *Esquire* magazine in a published letter entitled "Sour Drapes:"

"I used to think *Esquire* was cool, but your selections of The Ten Best-Dressed Jocks (August issue) make me think your fashion editor wears white socks and a key chain. Bob Gibson in that blue single-breasted looked just right for attending a funeral. . . ."

Frenchy was critical of the selections of Rod Gilbert and John Mackey and called Carl Eller's closet highlight a "Goodwill dashiki."

The letter concluded: "I do not know which is more embarrassing—to have been omitted, as I was, from your picks or to have been included among that motley crew. (Signed) Count Frenchy Fuqua, Running Back, Pittsburgh Steelers."

Frenchy's lack of haute couture recognition may have motivated him to his greatest season on the field and in the closet.

Teaming with Franco Harris and Terry Bradshaw in the Steeler backfield, Frenchy helped the Steelers win their first division championship in history in 1972. Frenchy also admits to leading Pittsburgh in any fashion parade. And for the third straight season, he is the Steeler "dress-off" champion.

One early morning Frenchy sat in his apartment sipping coffee and spilling his heart out. "I regret that I sent my

Count outfit back to Detroit, where I live in the off-season," he said, "it would have freaked you out. Skintight lavender jump suit with white buccaneer boots and pink floor-length cape and a monolithic glass cane. And, not finished yet, my white musketeer hat, turned up on the left side with pink, white and purple ostrich plumes. Wow! Oh, wow!

"Can you imagine that wacky magazine not including me, with an outfit like that? Next spring, know what I'm going to do? I will offer a formal challenge to all the so-called best-dressed in every city and send in the results to the magazine. Or have them cover the events!"

Frenchy's fiancée came in from the other room and he introduced her as "The Countess." She smiled. He went on. "The last time I was covered in a dress contest was for the Steelers. It's an annual thing and it's held about a month before the end of the season in the locker room after a practice.

"Everybody is fat-mouthin' about their rags until the moment of truth, when they meet the Count. Then they fall by the wayside. This year, Jim Clack was the white hope.

"You have all your clothes in your locker, hid. You put 'em on one at a time. We have an announcer who handles it like a prize fight. You start with the briefs. Clack broke out with powder-blue silk ones. I countered with my red bikinis.

"He pulled on some weird zebra stockings. Then I blew his mind, I laid my red panty hose on him.

"He broke back with some blue velour pants. I broke out in my pants with the new look of plaids. He tried to come on strong with some shirt that wasn't fantastic. He was fading, and I hadn't even got to the bulk of my dry goods. He knew it, because already I was getting the 'oohs' and 'aahs' from the players. He broke out in a plaid bow tie. Nothing. A sweater vest. Zero. Blue clogs. Embarrassing.

"I hit him with the rest of my three-piece red suit with blood-red turtleneck. Then I had a sensational gimmick.

From my vest pocket I pulled out a watch. I looked at it, looked at him, and replied, 'Your time is runnin' out, Clack.'

"Believe it or not, he began to sweat. He wiped his head with a towel. He said it was the lights."

Then Frenchy came on with his "Knockout stuff": three-inch high heel white boots, a white wool wrap-around monogrammed coat and "broke down my white, gangster-style hat on one side like only I can, and that was it."

"Clack knew he had been on the wrong track," said Frenchy. "He conceded. Right, Countess?" She smiled.

Frenchy continued on about his new caveman suit (with fur poncho) that he was soon to sport. ("Even my tailor gets carried away sometimes.") And how some of the players serve as his valet in the off-season (when he adds a few pounds and cannot bend in his skin-tight suits) and after games when they open doors for him and one may play a victory flute behind him.

"It's very exciting after games," he said. "I just feel good—when we win—from the top of my gorgeous head to the bottom of my curly toes. I hear the fans chanting when I come out of the locker room, 'Frenchy's comin', Frenchy's comin', what's he got on?' I sign autographs from different poses, so everyone can get a good look at me.

"Then I jump into my Mark IV. The Countess is waiting for me. I blast on a tape, usually a jumpin' tune like 'The Cisco Kid,' and we speed off. And, you know, this may sound silly, but like 50 yards away I can still hear the fans, 'Ooh, did you see that—was he *bad.*' "

I turned to Frenchy's fiancée (real name, Doris Moore) and asked her how she liked being "The Countess."

"It gives me a headache," she said.

George Sauer Incognito

February, 1974

George Sauer, Jr., never wanted this story told for fear it might crumble the ego of a certain Joe from Oberlin, O.

However, the bald details must now be exposed since George Sauer, Jr., after lying low the past few years, is in the news again in controversial fashion.

Sauer has announced that he plans to play for the Boston team of the embryonic World Football League. This causes a disruption among football aficionados for two reasons. One, Sauer is apparently still under contract to the New York Jets, a team he quit while still an All-Pro receiver four years ago, after the 1970 season.

The second reason for an emotional shuffle is that Sauer quit because he said football had become "dehumanizing" and "fascistic."

As for his Jet contract, only time and the law will tell. Regarding the second point, Sauer looks forward to playing for a respected and liked former teammate, Boston coach Babe Parilli. Also, the WFL, Sauer imagines, may be as pleasantly unpretentious and uncomputerized as the American Football League was when he first entered—and as the National Football League is not.

Mainly, though, Sauer at age 29 has never quite relieved himself of the itch to catch a pass.

This fellow named Joe can tell you that. So can a fellow named Cass Jackson.

Jackson is the head coach of the Oberlin College football team. Sauer, on a volunteer basis, was the assistant coach in charge of the offensive line. Now hear Jackson on Sauer, and Joe:

"I knew George still liked to play because when we both lived around San Francisco we'd toss the ball around in a park for three, four hours and then we'd stop and chat, and soon George would be up and running again, running pass patterns. He was like a kid. He almost wore my arm out.

"Sometimes we'd talk about the pros, and about all he'd say—and he mostly said it with his eyes—was, 'I wish it had been different, but it was fun while it lasted.'

"George stayed in shape. When he came to Oberlin to help me out, he was jogging five, six miles a day. And he watched his diet. Sometimes he'd have just a couple of glasses of orange juice for supper. And he kept his head in shape by reading Camus or James Joyce.

"Since I knew he still loved football I thought when he came to the Oberlin campus I'd take him out to play in the local sandlot pick-up game. It was funny. You had to see this to believe it.

"The local hotshots, all of us black, play every Sunday evening in summer. This is serious stuff, although we have fun. A lot of us were high school or college heroes. And I even played defensive back in the Canadian League.

"We play just below Oberlin hill, with trees on either side of the field. It's a beautiful setting, with the sun going down. And maybe a hundred people come out to watch—wives, girl friends, buddies, little kids.

"The week before I had brought an Oberlin philosophy teacher, who is white. It was embarrassing, he was so bad. He had been chosen on the team opposing mine, and after the game one of the guys whispered that I shouldn't bring back any more white dudes like that.

"During the next week, George arrives. I suggest he play

on Sunday. He says okay. I bring him out to the field and guys are giving me dirty looks. George doesn't look like much of a player. He's wearing a sweatshirt and black shorts and he's tossing the ball real loose. And he's wearing his glasses the way he does down on his nose.

"Nobody realizes this is George Sauer. I keep quiet just to see what happens.

"There are about 20 players. Sides are chosen and George isn't picked. But one of the guys on the other team tells me, if I want my friend to play he's got to be on my side. I say, well, okay.

"I throw the first pass of the game to George. It's an 80-yard touchdown. Nobody can believe what they've just seen, especially Joe, who is a star defensive player.

"He figures there was a slip-up somewhere. He says, 'I got this new cat.' The next play we run, George puts this fantastic move on Joe. George gets behind him, fakes toward the goal post. Joe lowers his head and starts chugging. George spins around and breaks to the sideline. I put the ball right on the money. Meanwhile, Joe is on the other side of the field. The crowd goes berserk.

"Now guys are on Joe. 'Hey, man, this cat's burnin' you up. Two TD's.' I figure now it's time, I got to fill 'em all in. 'This is George Sauer,' I say.

"The guys say, 'Whooo?' I say, 'George Sauer.' And again, 'Whoooo?' Someone says, 'Namath's receiver!' I say, 'Yeah.' And Joe pipes up, 'I got him.'

"So George scores four more touchdowns. We win 60-0. It became the biggest story of the season in the black neighborhood in Oberlin. Joe's a great athlete and he can laugh about it, too. He can even laugh at his new nickname. Everyone now calls Joe, 'I Got Him.' "

Larry Csonka: Monster?

November, 1971

When he was a high school senior, Larry Csonka was supposed to have nearly broken his house apart. He had been told that the way to strengthen a forearm was to keep banging away at something hard. "He smashed three walls and knocked one door off its hinges," said his father.

Years later Csonka was sleeping in a tent on a camping trip and was awakened by a neighborhood bear. Csonka reportedly elbowed the bear in the belly, and the intruder fled.

Before this season, Csonka, the Miami Dolphins' fullback, vowed that nothing short of a head injury would keep him out of the lineup. "If it's a broken bone or a muscle tear," he allegedly said, "I'd grab the doctor by the throat and say, 'Make it well, by God.' "

Then there is Larry Csonka on the field. Look: He is a 6-foot-2, 240-pound block of rock. His full face is dominated by a nose broken nine times over the years. Watch: Two Buffalo safeties at the five-yard line hit Csonka simultaneously from each side. They bounce off. Csonka enters the end zone standing up. Again: Csonka piles into mountain of Denver defenders, disappears, emerges out the other end to score, dragging defenders. And note: Midway through season Csonka leads American Football Conference in rushing.

"My brand of football is different from my life style, though a lot of people don't want to believe it," Csonka said. "I'm really an easygoing guy off the field. But everybody likes to promote the football player as a flesh-eating monster, dragging knuckles on the ground, wearing a beat-up sweater and sneakers that don't match."

Csonka is soft-spoken and articulate. He chooses his words carefully. A grunt does not seem to be in his vocabulary. His wife, Pam, says that Larry is usually very even-tempered at home. Larry also plays the harmonica to relax. None of which seems very flesh-eating or knuckle-dragging.

"Funny how stories grow," said Csonka. "Like the one about knocking walls down. That's not true. It was just one wall. It was in our kitchen. The wall had weak plaster. It wasn't that big a thing."

Does he still hit walls?

"Once in a while when I get angry. But doesn't everybody? Besides, I don't hit walls too hard any more," he said.

And what about the bear story?

"Nothing special. It was a small bear."

And the one about grabbing a doctor by the throat and demanding that an injury be made better immediately?

"Another exaggeration. I wouldn't grab anyone by the throat. Oh, sometimes you'd like to take hold of a defensive end and throttle him. But you don't. Football is so complicated, you've got to keep your cool to win. But I've found that you can hurt him just as much by impact, running smack into him."

Sometimes Csonka strikes back another way. He may be the only player in history to have been penalized 15 yards while carrying the ball. On that play he forgot that the tackler was not a wall and knocked him silly with a forearm.

"Every time a ball carrier runs he gets hit from 11 different directions," said Csonka. "And sometimes you've got 1,600 pounds of humanity crashing down on you. You've got to protect yourself.

"But football is very gratifying. Like when you're called

upon to go toe-to-toe in a tough, tight situation. I guess it dates back to prehistoric times, when mind and body combines to accomplish something special. And after it's through and you're so tired—well, it's like what Vince Lombardi said on the eve of his death, 'There's no better feeling than to lie on the field exhausted but victorious.'

"After football, I'm sure I'll never feel the same kind of satisfying self-expression again. I don't think you can ever feel that total mind-body exhilaration of accomplishment in the business world.

"Football is digging in and belting. I've enjoyed it since I was in junior high school in Stow, Ohio. I think about those days. We played on a dirt field behind the school. There were no bands at halftime. The only spectators were a few concerned parents. The bleachers were raggedy. So were our uniforms. They were old hand-me-downs from the high school. The right half of your shoulder pad usually didn't match the left half.

"We played hard because we loved it, and because we wanted to win. And until I began playing so much on artificial turf, I didn't realize how much fun dirt was. When I was a kid I really enjoyed the dirt in my ears and eyes. I guess I was always a dirty-faced kid.

"Yet I've always been concerned with the niceties. I mean, if I don't like what a person says, I probably wouldn't say anything because I wouldn't want to hurt his feelings.

"The only time I get mad off the field is, well, like when I get up in the middle of the night for a glass of water and I step on a sharp toy left by one of my little boys. Then I get excited. I jump around and holler obscenities.

"Or like when my car stalled three times in heavy traffic. The third time, I punched the dashboard. I broke the air conditioner. I also cut my hand open. I was bleeding all over the dash. I just sat there for 15 minutes feeling like a fool."

Joe Namath at Candlelight

Dorado Beach, Puerto Rico, February, 1972

Two women circle and stop and peek, like curious kittens, and ask themselves in quiet excitement, "Is that really . . . *him?*"

Joe Namath at dinner with three male companions raises a wine glass and toasts, "Health," when the two bejeweled middle-aged women interrupt. "Joe, may we bother you for an autograph for our sons?" One extends a cloth napkin.

Namath is giggly. He pushes back his chair, slowly rises. "Want me to write something special?" he asks. He laughs shyly, like a tickled schoolboy trying to cover a giggle from the teacher. "You won't get this napkin through customs," he says. The ladies are delighted.

Namath is one of the most immediately recognizable men in the United States, also one of the most controversial. Everyone has an opinion on Joe Namath, and it seems almost everyone wants his autograph, too.

Namath's mood is changed now from the time two years ago in 1970 when he received a crank threat on his life. He seemed more puzzled than frightened by such a vicious response to his carefree life style. For a time, it appeared he wanted to shrink from the limelight. But Namath is too spirited to remain hunched in dark corners.

One of Namath's dinner companions said he had recently talked with George Sauer, the former Jet who retired. "George said one reason he quit was that he was sick of people pawing and drooling over him because he was a football player," said the companion.

"George say that?" asked Namath. "Well, some people just don't want it. They don't like it. Steve Thompson wanted to go back home to work. So he up and quit the Jets, too."

Namath, his black hair in bangs, bent his head and dug into a steak. He looked up and smiled again, the candlelight on the table accentuating his deep dimples.

"I was supposed to have a date tonight," he said. "I met this beautiful blonde last night in the hotel casino here. I mean bee-yoo-tee-ful. I walked over to her and said, 'A beautiful woman like you shouldn't be alone.' She said she wasn't alone, exactly. But she didn't want to be with the guy she was with. I said, 'Well, that can be fixed.' She said not tonight. She was going back to her room—alone. I asked her about tomorrow night. She said yeah. I told her I'd call her at 6. I called. She wasn't in. I left a message. She never returned the call. I'd sure like to see her. I'd like to know what she was thinking about."

A man and his wife came over and got an autograph. They left.

"I noticed," said a dinner companion, "that you always stand when women come over to the table."

"Sure," Namath said. "That's the least I can do. I mean, if my mother asked for an autograph, I'd want the guy to stand for her."

His thoughts drifted to his home town, Beaver Falls, Pennsylvania.

"When I was in high school," he said, "a guy named Poolhead nicknamed me Joey U, 'cause I idolized Johnny Unitas. Those were the days. Did you know I worked one week as a shoeshine boy in a hat-cleaning store? They paid 50 cents a week. A week! I quit after the first week. I knew I was cut out for bigger things, even then." He pushed back his chair and bent over and laughed boyishly.

Joe came up for air, and his close friend and traveling companion, Becher Khouri, said, "I'll check the messages at the front desk, see if the girl called."

For all of the "Broadway Joe" headlines, Namath still seems to choose his friends the way he must have in Beaver Falls—are they straight? Are they loyal? Do they make him laugh? He mentioned a New York friend named Mickey. "He's in a couple small pizza restaurants with his father," said Namath. "I've known Mickey for several years, and I didn't know until recently that he never went past the ninth grade. I can dig that. I went to college, I told him, but I didn't learn much past the ninth grade anyway."

Khouri returns. No message from the blonde. Namath then pours more wine. More people come for autographs. The intermittent conversation rambles. Namath talks about how much he still admires Unitas and watches him on television whenever he can to steal some of the old master's tricks. "And he's still got 'em all," said Namath.

He asked about protesters he had recently read about. "People were picketing in New York about the Irish problems," he said. "I don't understand that. If people want to do something, why don't they just go to Northern Ireland and talk face-to-face with the people there who can do something about it? What good is picketing in New York?"

He lamented the theft of his $10,000 full-length mink coat from his New York apartment. "Funny thing is," he said, "I never wore it, I didn't pay for it. I got it for doing some P.R. But I loved it. I may buy another one."

He was laughing again, pouring more wine.

Just then, there was a tap on his shoulder. He turned. "I don't believe it, I don't believe it," he said into his napkin to muffle his surprise. He stood.

"Hello, Diane," said Joe. He pulled up a chair for her. It was the young woman with shoulder-length blond hair.

He sat back down and crossed his legs, leaned back in his seat, smiling quizzically at her. The flicker of the candle lit up his boyish blue eyes and he uttered a barely audible "wow."

Tom Dempsey: Star to Bum

Philadelphia, November, 1972

"Last year I was on top of the world," said Tom Dempsey. "Now I'm a bum."

During the 1970 season, New Orleans Saints fans shook the stadium with cheers for Tom Dempsey, inspirational hero. This season they threw tomatoes that splattered on his back and beer cans that clanked off his helmet. He was finally cut from the Saints and dropped out of football for six weeks. He was then placed on the taxi squad of the Philadelphia Eagles.

Tom Dempsey, yesterday's hero, is a field goal kicker. He is unique in his profession in that he was born with half a right foot. He must wear a special block-toe shoe. Some opponents last season even insisted that the shoe was an unfair advantage. Last year he kicked a 63-yard field goal for New Orleans to beat Detroit 19-17 in the closing seconds of play. It was the longest field goal in pro-football history, breaking a 14-year-old record by seven full yards.

Tom Dempsey became an instant national celebrity by his record kick. He was the shiningest example of a man overcoming adversity. In the off-season he received awards ranging from New Orleans American Legion Most Valuable Player to Pro Football Writers Most Courageous Player.

"A lot of people said I was cocky and that I stopped trying," said Dempsey. "That burns me up. I pushed harder than ever because I wanted to stay on top."

His problems began the first day of training camp this summer. Dempsey reported in at 265 pounds, 20 pounds more than coach J. D. Roberts had wanted him to carry.

"Tom worked hard to get the weight off, but it was tough," said Saints' publicity man Harry Humes.

In the exhibition season, Dempsey made but one field goal in eight attempts. Dempsey knew his job was in jeopardy. So did all the unemployed field goal kickers around the country. Like vultures, they smelled a dying carcass. About 20 kickers showed up in the Saints' camp. Dempsey said that the boos and the beer cans did not bother him. "They booed others, too," he said. "The fans in New Orleans are the greatest. Really. They're rabid. They pay eight dollars a game to see a job done, and they deserve the best. I guess I put too much pressure on myself to stay on top, and that screwed me up."

Dempsey was cut a week before the 1971 season started. Coach Roberts said that, yes, it was a little emotional, with Dempsey being crippled and a hero from last season. "You always feel a little bad when you have to fire someone."

Dempsey said that he was sure he'd come around soon, that it was a temporary slump. But Roberts has noted that Dempsey has never in his four-year pro career been a consistent kicker, even though he led the Saints in scoring the last two years. Last season, despite three field goals from past 50 yards, Dempsey was 11th best out of the 13 regular field goal kickers in the National Football Conference. His kicks were good 53 percent of the time. Curt Knight, who led the league, had a 74 percent field goal kicking average.

Dempsey, last season's hero, began selling insurance in New Orleans. He was hurt and embarrassed. "I was married in June," he said, "and I thought my wife married a hero. Now I was thinking she married a washout. But she stuck behind me."

Dempsey continued to kick nights at a nearby park. He would chase the ball himself. And he continued to call teams, trying to hook on somewhere. One day, six weeks after he was cut by New Orleans, the Eagles said they had a job open on the taxi squad.

A member of the taxi squad does not suit up for games, does not make road trips, is not on the roster. He practices with the team, which means, in the case of kicking specialists, that he goes off by himself. Kickers are the quirks of football teams. Noncontact players in a contact sport. Dempsey is there just in case, in case regular kicker Happy Feller starts missing or is injured.

"You go through a year like I went through," said Dempsey, "going from the top to the bottom, and you know that football is a plastic world, a fantasy land. And you come to realize that there are more important things in the world than football. You come to value your home life, for example, and feel lucky that you've married the right woman. But I still love the game. And I still think I'm a good kicker. I still think I can kick in this league."

In the following seasons, Dempsey became the Eagles' star kicker.

Andy Russell: Whatever Happened to Superman?

December, 1973

Andy Russell says he stopped taking drugs to improve his play five years ago and then virtually had to "relearn the game."

Russell, now in his ninth season as a Pittsburgh Steeler linebacker, said that from his rookie season in 1963 until

Chuck Noll became the team's head coach in 1969, he took an amphetamine, commonly called the "pep pill," before nearly every National Football League game he played.

"It made me think I was invincible when I was on the field," says Russell today. "I felt I was playing with a great flair and was very courageous.

"Then on Tuesday I would watch the game films, and I was shocked to see that I didn't play anything like I thought I played. I was just another guy out there doing a job. No superman at all."

In 1969, several things happened to change Russell's drug life. First, one of Noll's earliest moves as coach, says Russell, was to forbid drug usage on the team. Secondly, Noll's concept of defense emphasized a cool discipline; the pep pills, said Russell, "made me play with more reckless abandon. And so now I had to calm down, I couldn't shoot the gaps as much—I just about had to learn to play the game all over again."

Russell plays the game as well as anyone in pro football. Last season, for example, he was named All-American Football Conference by both wire news services and the *Sporting News*. He is a Pro Bowl regular.

He is certainly one of the most sensitive, highly regarded athletes in professional sports. Last season he was awarded the Whizzer White Humanitarian award "for outstanding contribution to his team, community, and country." Russell is the Steeler player representative and defensive captain. He is head of the Players' Association committee on safety and health.

And despite his ominous 'stache and violent occupation, there is a soft, amiable look in his eyes.

Russell, who began taking drugs in college, says "When I first came into the league, I'd say that a majority of the players took drugs." He believes that fewer and fewer football players are taking drugs today. Several reasons for that.

One is the league rule that if you're caught popping pills, you get an automatic suspension. That's stiff.

"Another reason is that players are beginning to understand that pills can be destructive to your performance. I think they were to mine. I made some spectacular plays, but I also made more mistakes than I do now. People don't often realize how complicated football can be, and it doesn't lend itself to total recklessness."

Russell also contends that veterans took drugs as a way of life. Younger players today have a different view of things.

"I can only speak for the Steelers, at least my knowledge and experience with some of the players on the Steelers. After all, I don't know what everyone does. And even in the days when I was popping pills, I did it surreptitiously, hiding my head in my locker or going into the latrine. I felt guilty. I knew the league didn't sanction it, even then.

"But younger players, like a Jack Ham and a Mike Wagner, grew up wanting to be pro football players—as opposed to older guys who just happened to become pros. The younger guys watched the pros on television, they got more caught up in taking care of one's body for the purpose of being a pro.

"I guess they learned that popping pills could be destructive, or habit-forming, or a fake high. So they started into fantastic body-building stuff. When I was in high school or college and guys did that, we'd consider them narcissistic S.O.B.'s."

Russell's opinions come on the heels of contrary views by the California State Board of Medical Examiners who said, while investigating the habits of the San Diego Chargers, that "the condition (of pill taking on the Chargers) is worse today than in October 1969," when the NFL forbade the random distribution of drugs by team trainers. Team doctors were put in charge.

Russell's observations also differ from those of George

Burman of the Washington Redskins who recently said that one-third to one-half of the Redskins regularly take drugs.

"I have respect for George," said Russell, "and I'm sure he thinks he is right. But how does he know? He can't see everyone. And sometimes, even when guys say something, they might be kidding. Guys will say, 'I'm really going to get up for next week's game. I'm starting on my bennies on Wednesday.' Or they'll lift up a giant ashtray to their mouth and say, 'This is the latest in bennies.'

"On the other hand, the Redskins are a veteran team—the 'over-the-hill' mob. And as I said, I think veterans are generally more dependent on drugs than younger players.

"You do hear a lot of rumors in football. We used to hear stories about the Chargers. Well, when Houston Ridge sues and wins $300,000 because of drug abuse on the Chargers, there must be some substance to the rumors.

"But in almost 10 years in the pros, about the only guy I ever saw take a pill was Chuck Beatty, a defensive back. This was in 1969. We were playing in Philadelphia. We had a bad team and this was going to be our final game of the season. No play-offs.

"Before the game, Chuck takes out a bottle from his dop kit and in front of everyone casually pops a pill. One of the assistant coaches sees it, comes running and screaming to Chuck. "What are you doing? You know that's illegal! What's wrong with you!'

"The locker room was quiet as a tomb. Then Chuck says, 'Aw Coach, I was only taking the pill because I got a long drive home after the game, and I want to be sure I stay awake.' "

Muhammad Ali and the Fly

Chicago, July, 1971

A couple of flies did midair imitations of the Ali shuffle as the original, Muhammad Ali himself, sat in the motel lobby talking with a companion. One fly alighted on the right knee of Ali.

"See that fly? Mind that fly," said Ali, his conversational tone interrupted by his whisper. His large left hand began to creep out. His eyes were fixed on the fly.

"You gotta know how to do it," he said, barely moving his lips. "The fly is facing me and he can only fly forward. Now, I come forward and turn my hand back-handed. It's like a left jab."

Ali struck. Then he brought his fist in front of the man seated next to him. "Watch this," said Ali. He slowly opened his hand. Ali looked up wide-eyed. "Thought I had him," he said. "My timing's off."

Ali was in training for a fight with Jimmy Ellis. This was shortly after the announcement that the Supreme Court had overturned his conviction for refusing the draft.

"It's hard to train now," he said. "I got bigger things on my mind, bigger things than just beatin' up somebody. Fighting's not the thing any more for me. I see myself fighting for another year, at most. I'll have one more fight with Joe Frazier.

"Then I got obligations to keep. I want to help clean up black people. I want to help respect black women. I want to help the wine-heads in the alleys. I want to help the little black kids in the ghettos. I want to help in narcotics programs. I want to serve the honorable Elijah Muhammad (the head of the Black Muslim religion, of which Ali is a minister, though temporarily suspended).

"Fighting is just two brutes beatin' on each other. A man goes through certain stages in his life. Fightin' was a joy to me at one time, now it's work. I don't even like for anybody to see me doing roadwork. But I remember when I first turned pro in 1960, I was in Florida and I was going to write the name Floyd Patterson on my jacket. To trick the people, to make them think I was the champ when I was runnin' alongside the highway. I wanted to show off."

Ali was suspended by Elijah Muhammad because Ali continued as a fighter, a profession supposedly anathema to the religion. But Ali has been a boxer since he was a boy in Louisville. And he needs money to pay alimony to his first wife and also to pay the astronomical legal fees which have piled up in the last four years as he fought his draft case.

Ali swiped at another fly. Missed. He tried again. Missed. And again. Same result. One more. Nothing.

"You've missed five times," said the companion.

Ali looked embarrassed. "Five?" he repeated.

"These flies keep flying 'round me," he said. "They must know I'm not all I used to be. They must see the little gray hairs that been growin' in my head lately.

"If Ellis is as quick as these flies, I'm in trouble."

A man approached and asked for Ali's autograph for two boys. "Their mother has trouble making them clean their room," the man said.

Ali wrote: "To Timmy and Rickie. From Muhammad Ali. Clean that room or I will seal your doom." Ali smiled at his spontaneous doggerel, the man laughed, thanked him.

The implied threat to the boys was in keeping with his easy wit, his breezy charm, the bluster that too many people have taken too seriously over the years. His still-smooth face and, now, subdued yet animated ways seem to belie his vicious profession. And when he refused to enter the draft, saying, "I ain't got no quarrel with them Viet Cong," many held that he was being hypocritical. A fighter is a fighter, they held, whether in the ring or in the rice paddies.

A fly again landed on his knee. Ali suddenly grew still. He slowly reached out to snatch the fly. Jabbed. Had it! "My timing's back!" cried Ali. "See, at least I'm not *too* old."

He dropped the fly to the carpet. The fly didn't move.

"He's staggered," said Ali, proudly, bending down. "That's a science, y'know. To stagger the fly and not to kill him. You get him in your hand, but you don't squeeze."

Ali flicked the fly with his index finger. "Go on, fly, fly away. I don't want to kill him. Let him live like us."

The fly flew off.

Joe Frazier at Dawn

Philadelphia, February, 1971

Joe Frazier's day begins in the dark, in Fairmount Park. The blue-black morning is damp with drizzle and already soggy with carbon monoxide from some early autos on the road. Joe's chauffeur-driven Cadillac limousine creeps behind him with bug-eyed lights.

A long undulating shadow is cast downroad and bobs in eerie rhythm to the Army-booted scraping of Joe Frazier's jogging. The rhythm is relentless even when a big twig, snapped underfoot, issues a sharp report.

To Joe's right is one sparring partner, Ken Norton. In back of the car is another, Moleman Williams. Suddenly, from behind a black bend emerges a hooded man. He jogs past, tosses up a cursory wave.

"How ya doin', daddy?" asks Frazier rapidly. A nod, no reply.

Frazier has been up and running at 5:30 in the morning for six weeks now, in preparation for his heavyweight championship bout with Muhammad Ali on March 8.

He has returned to Philadelphia from the Catskills because the cold was 17 degrees below zero, the snow 17 inches high, the mountain roadwork treacherous, and the beads of sweat froze like black pearls on his face.

But Spartan routine must be adhered to. The pain of tedium and fatigue must be respected, accepted, and pursued. So Joe Frazier runs even when his sparring partners cannot stir from within womblike blankets. He does not like to run alone, for that compounds the hollowness of his solitary profession. And the hour before daybreak is of primeval isolation. Yet Joe's schedule waits for no man.

Imperceptibly, a wash of gray has changed night into day. Now, in a little blue pinstriped railroad cap cocked a bit cockeyed on his skull and gold sweat jacket with upturned collar and blue sweat pants, Joe has lost his shadow. Headlights off; wipers on.

He grunts, snorts. Perspiration streaks with rain. His black, flat-nosed face glistens.

"We don't talk much," said Ken Norton later. "Just some idle talk to pass the boredom. Sometimes Joe'll ask me how much time left."

Without breaking stride, Norton calls to the driver, Les Pelemon (also assistant trainer and lead singer in Joe's rock group, "The Knockouts"). Whatever time Les says, Norton relates, Joe grumbles. "I think you wanna buy another watch," says Joe.

Sometimes another car will come by and slow up and the driver looks. But mostly there is only the wet, caped statue of

General Grant; the quill-poised statue of Lincoln, bearded like Frazier; barren trees; mud-gray gullies; the Undine Barge Club along the Schuylkill River; a long sculler escaping a wake of water in the dawn.

They have run 28 minutes, nearly three miles, almost 10 rounds. They are about done.

"Muhammad's hurtin'!" cries Norton. "Two minutes to go! He's on the ropes. Let's go git 'em!"

The two take off in a sprint. Shortly, Ken shouts, "He just fell."

End of roadwork.

Frazier went on to win a unanimous decision over Ali.

Marcel Cerdan, Jr., and Shadow

Kiamesha Lake, New York, May, 1970

A longer than full-length mirror on the wood-paneled wall and Marcel Cerdan, Jr. (always *Junior*) jiggles in front of it, flicking short combinations with distended pinkies, lightly toe-dancing in black sweat socks and black Adidas and one wonders what he sees when he looks into the mirror.

He believes in visions and mysticism and superstitions. In dreams before nearly every bout, he says he sees the ghost of his father, the former middleweight champion who died in a plane crash in the fog-drenched Azores mountains in 1949. He still wears his father's wristwatch before every bout (his father wore two wristwatches as a superstition, too, and the discovery of one of them denoted that he was not one of the plane's survivors) and carries with him the blood-stained trunks Cerdan senior wore when he beat Tony Zale for the title 22 years ago.

And in Paris, before each fight, young Cerdan kisses the photograph on the gravestone of Edith Piaf, sentimental chanteuse, who was his father's mistress in an internationally known love affair.

Before the mirror his wrinkled forehead begins to fill with sweat in his training quarters at the Concord Hotel here in the Catskill Mountains, as he prepares for a welterweight fight against Donato Paduano in Madison Square Garden. Does he see his father in the mirror? Or his father's son?

Or does he see just Marcel Cerdan, Jr., 26 years old, 5 foot 7, an unlikely looking prizefighter except for the nose as flat as a peppermint leaf and a stern, intense countenance.

There is a boyish look about him, and only when he tugs on the headgear and peers out with dark eyes is pugnacity hinted.

His skin is pale as an Irish schoolboy's and not very hairy. Neither his arms nor legs ripple with muscle. His waist is undefined and he wears a rubber belt during workouts to keep it trim as possible. He pinches his tummy a lot after workouts, the way a baker does with dough. His legs are knock-kneed.

Reputation as a puncher does not precede him, as it did his father. But sparring with blood-red gloves he demonstrated quickness of hand and leg and head-bob that moved Johnny Condon, the Garden's natty publicity man (and not altogether impartial), to note, "He doesn't look like a fighter who can't fight. I saw his old man, and he couldn't move that way."

In France, Cerdan senior is still revered. Frenchmen supposedly are "daring" young Cerdan to be, if not equal to his father, then simply outstanding.

"I idolize my father more than anyone does," said Cerdan, Jr., through a translator. "I will never be as good as my father, no. It is unfair to ask anyone to be as great as him. But I must be very good."

As an amateur he won 37, lost two, drew one. Since turning pro at 21, he is undefeated in 47 fights, with one tie. He has been charged with "not having fought anybody."

Paduano, also undefeated, is "somebody." If Cerdan wins, "maybe then my people will accept me."

The memory of his father is all around. Not far from here (at Evans Lodge), his father trained for the Zale fight and hid Miss Piaf and her lady friend in a cold, dank, deserted bungalow for fear of scandal, and each night sneaked food under his jacket in the dark of the moon to his inamorata.

At the training table here, Johnny Condon had somehow located a button, like a campaign button, with a face that resembled closely that of Marcel Cerdan, Jr.

"It must be 25 years old, that button," said Johnny.

"Hoooo," said young Cerdan, eyes growing wide, "papa." And he pinned it on his jacket.

Cerdan lost to Donato by a decision. Three years later, Marcel Cerdan, Jr., was a retired boxer.

Rodriguez's Madness

New York, April, 1971

Chi Chi Rodriguez tries to be a clown in the finest fresh-air funeral parlors in the world—golf courses, where "shh" is the shibboleth. He was a poor Puerto Rican who worked in sugar fields as a boy and now works in places where people talk with invisible clothespins clipped on their noses.

Rodriguez is a slight man who has outdriven Jack Nicklaus who has outdriven Paul Bunyan. Rodriguez feels he represents Puerto Rico in "a gentleman's manner," yet was fined $250 by the PGA for "actions detrimental to his fellow competitor."

"That hurt him very deeply but he didn't show it," said his wife, Iwalani. "Spanish people are very sensitive."

She said that "clamps have been put on Chi Chi" since then. "He can't dance on the greens any more, he can't cover the hole with his hat any more," she said. "But he still does clown. He thinks golf should be fun, and he thinks the gallery should get something for its money."

Rodriguez has been on the tour since 1960, and sometimes there are grumblings among fellow pros about his shenanigans. But when Dave Hill, his playing partner during one round of last October's Kaiser Open, asked him to save his joyful ravings for *after* the hole, Rodriguez became incensed. "I'll fight you right here," said Rodriguez.

His problems increased at the turn of the year. He underwent an operation for a tennis elbow in November and had a growth removed from the palm side of his left thumb. So he continues with renewed health his quest to be "the greatest golfer in the world." He has not won a tour tournament since 1968, though he won $53,000 last year.

"Chi Chi's trouble," said one pro, "is that he read his press clippings and believed that he was the most powerful small man ever. Now, he practically falls down trying to hit the ball so hard."

But he is back tramping up a fairway hill with elbows jigging in minuscule imitation of Jackie Gleason's "Away we go." To the chagrin of some. Golf courses are sullen places. A golfer stroking demands the solemnity of last rites. A cough from the gallery sounds to a tense golfer like a car backfiring. But Rodriguez elicits laughter.

He hits a long shot: "Ain't bad for a little Puerto Rican."

About his size: "You should have seen how little I was as a kid. I was so small that I got my start in golf as a ball marker."

Rodriguez likes to say he has no set routines, that he is totally spontaneous. But a caddy nearby notes: "The same old corn."

And once in the press tent of the Masters, after a fine round, he was going over his day hole by hole, with quips. The accommodating press laughed heartily. Near the end, quizzically, honestly, and a little sadly, he asked, "Do you really think I'm funny?"

"I don't think I'm a funny man," said Rodriguez recently, "I'm just happy." His wife relates that the first thing he does in the morning is sing. But he admits that he is a nervous man. "Because I work too hard," he said. He is assiduous about exercises that help give him the strength at 5 feet 7½ inches tall and 130 pounds to drive balls 300 yards.

At 35, with an outline of gray hair at the nape of his neck, he still has the jounce of youth. When he receives applause after a good shot, he holds up two fingers, in the contemporary show of communal peace. "I love the new generation," he said. "They have more of a smile than the old."

He says he will probably play 10 more years on the tour, and then would like to go back to Puerto Rico and build a golf course so young, poor kids can play for free on it. Maybe, too, he said, he would like to run for governor. "My idea is not to be a big shot, but to make the poor people big shots."

"Chi Chi always wants to help people," said his wife, Iwalani. "He wants to be liked so much."

Frank Beard's Melodrama

Iowa City, August, 1973

After a year-and-a-half of a slump so horrible he felt he was on the brink of death ("melodramatic but true"), Frank Beard sees a rainbow at the end of the fairway.

The allusion to death was in psychological terms, says Beard, and the erosion of his golf game attacked his pride, attacked his masculinity and attacked his notions of his own infallibility.

"Nothing in my life had prepared me for bad times," said Beard, as he walked, talked, tossed grass into the air to measure the wind, and whacked a number of handsome shots in the pro-am golf tournament here. "My whole career had been straight up. My basic problem was that I had never had a problem before. I didn't know how to cope with it. I never built up an immunity to disaster."

In 11 years on the professional golf tour, the 34-year-old Beard had become one of the finest players and a money-winner to rank alongside Palmer, Nicklaus, Trevino, Casper, and Player. In 1969, he led all golfers with earnings of $175,224. But in 1972 he was the 40th on the money-winners list, his worst finish since his first full year on the tour, in 1963.

He had begun to experiment with hitting the ball straight instead of hooking it, as he had always done. One bad round led to another. He soon repaired the mechanical aspect of his game but now his confidence was creaking.

"I began to fear," he said. "Once, I just approached the ball and knew I would hit it right. Now, I began to ask myself, 'Can I do it?' A champion never asks himself that question. It's paralyzing.

"I began to fear playing bad, feared what people might say. But I wouldn't admit fear, and so I kept on, with my confidence devastated. I was like a dope addict or an alcoholic. I couldn't belly up to my problem.

"Maybe the most important reason I wouldn't face it was that it attacked my manhood. Me, afraid? No! Can't be."

Beard had been an outstanding athlete all his life and had once even considered professional baseball as a career. His brother, Ralph, was an all-American basketball player. His father, though, was a teaching pro and both saw greater financial possibilities in golf. Everything, until recently, had gone according to form.

Like many athletes, Beard had defined himself in terms of athletic success. Shoot below par, you are a good and worthy human being. Mess up on the putting green and you're a worm.

"It was a syndrome of your seeing yourself and others seeing you for what you did instead of for what you are," said Beard.

"That hurts, but it's true. When I began to play lousy the phone stopped ringing as much as it used to. But there were a few friends who stayed with me, who asked my wife and me to dinner not because I was Frank Beard the Golfer, but because we were the Beards and they enjoyed our company.

"Until I came to the realization, and it was a gradual thing, that golf is not the most important thing in my life, that there are other things to live for, until then I thought I was really on the brink of death—if I hadn't died already and nobody had informed me."

Beard says he has gone through what for him are drastic changes. On the outside, his brown but graying hair is longer, his pants are slightly bell-bottomed, his shirts are blue, red, green, and not always white as they once were. "I may still be drab to most people, but to me this is practically going to hell," he said.

And inside, the changes are manifold. For one, he says, "I'm not chasing the buck the way I used to. Once, if I went home supposedly to relax instead of going to a tournament, I'd be reading the papers and saying, 'There's $150,000 in prize money, and I'm not going to get any of it.' And when I'd read who won, I'd say, 'I could have beaten his butt.' I might as well have been at the tournament. Now, I still follow the tournament when I'm home but I don't agonize as much. I spend that time enjoying my family."

He has recently gone on another of his many diets. "I figured if I can't control myself at the table how could I expect to control myself on the golf course," he said. The 6-foot Beard went from 205 pounds to 180. The intelligent, solidly good-looking face with wire-rimmed glasses is not as round as previously.

"The confidence and stroke are just about back completely," said Beard. He said this shortly after he had finished ninth at the Firestone. "It was about 20 spots higher than I had been finishing."

"But I never gave up the faith," he continued. "It never occurred to me that I wouldn't play well tomorrow. And I did have a few good rounds that kept my hopes up—and also contributed to my letdowns.

"I look back on all this and I have to believe it was the best year-and-a-half of my life," said Beard. "It attacked my manhood but it made me more of a man."

Steve Mizerak: Happy Hustler

July, 1974

The man who admits to being the best pool player in the world was demonstrating some common, everyday miraculous trick shots to a few friendly acquaintances, including writer and pro tyro George Plimpton, in whose Manhattan home these wonders occurred.

Steve Mizerak, U.S. Open pocket billiards champion for the last four years, lined up three balls at the front end of the table. He put one ball in front of one corner pocket, and one ball in front of the other corner pocket, and one ball against the edge in the middle.

He said he would knock in one ball, have the cue ball spin around the middle ball and knock the far ball in the second pocket. He did.

Small potatoes. He had about 20 other tricks up his stick. He virtually had the balls hopping in one pocket and out into another. The balls became rotund automatons that scooted where told.

Now, Mizerak lined up four balls in a row directly in front of a side pocket. The cue ball was set up in front of the other side pocket. "I will knock in the ball closest to the pocket without the cue ball touching the front three balls," he announced.

"Impossible," muttered Plimpton. Pause. "But I won't bet on it."

A cloud of drama gathered momentum in the room.

Mizerak, blondish, heftyish, and mysteryish, tread scientifically around the table, casing the joint. Finally, he set, he hunched, he squinted, he aimed in pendulum fashion and stroked softly.

As the cue ball headed slowly on its mission, Mizerak swept aside balls one, two and three with his stick. The cue ball, like a halfback following perfect blocking, knocked in the front ball. The tricky trick shot had been performed just as Mizerak had said, but to the groans of his friends.

Mizerak is 29 years old and has been amazing people with his billiard artistry ever since he began hanging out in a pool hall at age four. The pool hall in Steve's case was the safest place for him since his father, who owned the smoke-embalmed emporium, could keep a fastened eye on the tot.

From such humble but netherworldly beginnings in Perth Amboy, New Jersey, Steve Mizerak went on to reap some fame, some fortune, and some danger.

He recalls one tingly afternoon in Nashville, Tennessee, while on a business tour through various billiards nests in the South. He had sallied forth from Athens College in Athens, Alabama. His baggage included one cue stick and one fellow collegian, a mountainous wrestler.

Mizerak was beating the owner of the pool hall when the owner's wife hollered from behind the counter, "Honey, if you cain't win from this feller, then we'll have to just shoot his tail off."

"I walked over to my muscleman," Mizerak recalls, "and said, 'If she pulls a gun, what'll you do?'

"He said, 'What should I do?' That's when I knew I was in trouble. Well, I won and we ran."

Perhaps this is why Mizerak has been so successful in the last four U.S. Opens. He can relax.

"Sometimes that's hard to do, too," he said. "I mean, say a guy is running a hundred balls on you, and it's happened to me more than once. You want to jump up and bite the guy's hand. But all you are allowed to do is sit and stare. It's horrible."

What's almost as miserable, if you're one of the 100 or so "legitimate" professional billiards players in the United States (and it's here that the best billiards in the world is played), is that you earn starvation wages even if you are the best.

In 1974, Mizerak was the number one money-winner with about $8,500 in prize money—$6,000 coming from the U.S. Open win alone. He had to supplement that income in order to feed and shelter his family—wife and three-year-old boy—by teaching seventh-graders geography and spelling; owning his own pool parlor (all neat and socially acceptable); writing a book, *Inside Pocket Billiards* (Regnery); and as a paid adviser to the Brunswick staff.

Luther Lassiter, whom Mizerak beat for the title, pumps gas in North Carolina when not behind the eight ball.

However, Mizerak says he never has to do any anonymous touring of pool joints anymore. "Funny," he said, "but if you go into a place and tell them who you are—they want to play you anyway. I imagine they're proud to go home and tell their wives, 'Hey, Sadie, guess what, I just lost 20 bucks to the national champ.' "

Reflecting on his checkered career in and out of the nation's pool halls, posh (like the grand ballroom of the Sheraton-Chicago Hotel where the U.S. Open championship is held) or otherwise, Mizerak said:

"There has always been the feeling in this country that kids should not go into pool halls because of the bad influence of the so-called bums that are hanging out. But I don't know, I learned a lot from talking to all those guys."

And what, he was asked, did he learn?

With a hint of a hustler's smile, he said after a short thought, "I guess I learned what not to do."

Bobby Fischer: Sportin' Champ

New York, January, 1972

Dripping wet—which made his long, bony face look even longer—hunched and barefoot and blue-robed, Bobby Fischer came out of the shower to answer the door.

One o'clock in the afternoon, but his small hotel room was dark behind him. Curtains were drawn. No lights on except for the one from the bathroom. "Sorry," said Fischer, to his expected visitor, "just got up a few minutes ago. Be with you right away." He padded back to the bathroom, closed the door. Pitch black. The visitor stood for a surprised moment in the darkness, then fumbled along the wall for the light switch.

Mysterious and controversial, famous and infamous, one-time child prodigy and current U.S. chess champion, Bobby Fischer lives in hotel rooms. He has no permanent residence. For now, this Park-Sheraton room is also his training field. Some time before June 30, Fischer will challenge the reigning world chess champion, Boris Spassky of the Soviet Union, for the title.

"It will be," Fischer will say later, "probably the greatest sports event in history. Bigger even than the Frazier-Ali fight. It is really the free world against the lying, cheating, hypocritical Russians."

Fischer's live-in training field is spare. Two single beds, one rumpled, take up much of the space. A TV set in the corner. An alarm clock on the bedstand. No clothes are strewn about. On the made bed is a small, open satchel. In it are some papers and four magazines: *U.S. News & World Report, Esquire, The Plain Truth* (a Bible-oriented news magazine), and *Playboy.*

On the desk are the tools of his trade, the tools of his single passion, the tools that, as a *New York Times* music critic has written, Fischer employs with a genius that is as unique as Beethoven's; on the desk is a chessboard. The "board" is actually a kind of soft plastic, the chess pieces are wooden but almost weightless. Convenient to carry wherever he goes. A book of chess moves called *Chess Informant,* in seven languages, is open. There are marks alongside some of the games, and marginal notes. Fischer stays up late going over past games, historical games, Spassky's games.

Quickly, he puts on a dark maroon suit, white shirt and a maroon tie that says *Playboy* on it and is interspersed with bunny symbols.

All dressed, he returned to the bathroom, then popped out a few minutes later. His face was covered with shaving cream, "Say, would you mind putting the chain on the door. The maid or somebody might walk in," he said.

Shaved, he showed upon request a particularly "dumb" move he saw in one of the games from the book. "But don't write what the move is," said Fischer. "I don't want to leak anything to the Russians." His fingers are long and he jabs a piece down, making the others twitch. He was also proud of the chess set. "Look at these pieces," he said. "Smooth and light, no hard edges, beautifully carved. The best set for playing that I've ever seen. Here, feel this knight."

He talked about chess as a sport.

"Sure, it's a sport," he said. "And when newspapers put it in entertainment and arts sections, that's downgrading chess, completely out of place.

"You've got to be in top condition to play chess. You have

to concentrate in a tournament for five hours at a time, day after day. And when there's an adjournment, you've got to stay up late analyzing strategy. The tension and the need for stamina are brutal. One mental lapse and you're through. That's why a lot of great chess players are over the hill by 40. Too old for the strain.

"Spassky even has a physical trainer. I do my own physical conditioning. I don't eat fatty foods. I keep my weight at 180 pounds. I like to exercise with the Jack LaLanne Show. He's got a fun personality. I play tennis, too. Not too good, though. But I like the new metal racquets. Now I can even get the ball over the net sometimes." He laughed. "I've begun to bowl, that's a great sport. Jogging? No, jogging is too dull.

"I'd compare chess to basketball. Basketball players pass the ball around until they get an opening. Like chess, like the mating attack."

His brown eyes widened. He laughed. Back to the Spassky match. A place and exact time have not yet been set. "But the buildup will be terrific," said Fischer. "Like the Ali-Frazier fight, though I don't approve of boxing; I think it's immoral." He said, though, that he admires Ali as an athlete. Which other athletes does he admire?

"I don't follow sports much, except when it's news—like Lee Trevino, when he won these Opens and was on the covers of *Time* and *Newsweek*. But I like Willie Mays a lot. Like his basket catch. He gives all he's got. He's not one of those sluggards. He loves the game.

"I grew up in Brooklyn, was a Dodger fan. I liked Don Newcombe because he was a good hitter. He wasn't satisfied with being only a good pitcher, like most pitchers.

"I like Joe Namath. I think he's got class. He sacrifices himself. A champion needs that. He's got these terrible knees and probably should be retired. But when he plays he is not worried about being hit, getting the ball off is all important.

"Too many times, people don't try their best. They don't have the keen spirit, the winning spirit. And once you make it, you've got to guard your reputation—every day go in like an unknown to prove yourself. That's why I don't clown around. I don't believe in wasting time. My goal is to win the world's chess championship to beat the Russians. I take this very seriously."

Fischer beat Spassky, decisively.

Rod Laver at the Office

New York, January, 1971

And, finally, in the last cadenza of the practice session, in the way a champion prize fighter thrums the speed bag, Rod Laver asked his teen-aged mate if he'd throw some lobs for the final five minutes of the hour.

Laver became a ruddy blur and chased what seemed like a thousand tennis balls in every corner of the court at once.

Rod Laver is more powerful that he has any right to be. With a puffy, resplendent crown of red hair and a sharp beak, he dominates a tennis court the way a rooster rules a barnyard. He seems to squeeze every last kilogram of energy from his smallish body, the way archy the cockroach typed. Archy, the poet roach of Don Marquis's imagination, typed by plunging full force on the typewriter keys. His muscles were not developed enough, however, to use the shift key for capitals and punctuation. That's where archy and Laver differ.

Laver stands 5 foot 9 and weighs 150, but he is nonetheless a goodly physical specimen, with emphasis on his left arm, which seems nearly double the size of his right. He guesses his left wrist is about an inch-and-a-half larger than his right.

The game is a business with Laver, and even in practice his concentration is deep. Last year he made over $200,000 in tournament prize money. This year he may even make more. He says that practice is work, but that he enjoys his work and that he cannot afford to slouch any time he grips a racket in his freckled fingers.

"That would be bad business, wouldn't it?" he asks rhetorically.

Workout this day was held inside the Vanderbilt Club in New York, which has two tennis courts that are sheathed in lime-green drapes. Laver and Dick Stockton, a Trinity College player and unranked amateur, came onto one court as a quartet of ladies was leaving.

"Have a nice game, ladies?" asked Laver, in polite Australian lilt.

On the court, in white satiny jacket and pants, Laver began to uncreak. He had laid off tennis for a few days. Now he just wanted to hit the ball in the middle of the racket and to harness that right rhythm, the kind of rhythm that allows an athlete to perform without effort—no, to perform without *conscious* effort. "So that you are not pulling against your body," says Laver.

He began a stream of conversation with himself (sarcastic: "Oh, that's a good shot, Rod"), with the ball ("You rotten ball"), with the racket (haughty: "The ball too high for you?"), with the net ("Hitting your tape enough?") and with Stockton who makes a good shot ("Rat!").

After almost half an hour of work on the base line, at the net, with various services, Laver says, "Take a couple serves, Dick, and we'll have a game."

It has been very much like a boxer's workout, where a

fighter will practice various aspects of his craft—counter-punches, jabs, footwork, weaves. Now the game begins, like a spar match. It is evident, too, what the spectator attraction for tennis singles is. It possesses the satisfaction of head-to-head competition of a prize fight without the bloodshed.

Laver believes tennis will be the sport of the '70s. He said that tennis courts are sprouting up all over the country and that they are even being built instead of swimming pools for private homes. The interest in Open tennis and the fact that it could be a family sport, and that Americans are becoming more family oriented, he said, are other reasons for the tennis growth.

Laver, his red hair darkening from sweat, began to assume his mastery. He lined shots an inch over the net and an inch from the right sideline, an inch from the left. (Said Stockton, later, "My god, he's marvelous. To think I was playing with the best player in the world. It blows your mind.")

Then workout's end, with Laver flying every which way for Stockton's lobs and, finally, one final slam by Laver, the crescendo.

A Few Kicks Left

Near the end of his career, the athlete still has some trouble adjusting to life at twilight. And, as archy the roach said with melancholy encouragement to his friend, mehitabel the cat, "there's a dance in the old dame yet."

Pancho Gonzales: The Old Lion

New York, September, 1974

Most old lions, on a sultry Sunday afternoon, would wish to crawl into tall, cool grass and loll away the rest of the day.

And so it seemed for Pancho Gonzales, the tawny, ferocious tennis king of years gone by. Fittingly, Gonzales slumped on two folding chairs in the shade of the Forest Hills grandstand, his tennis socks and belly both slightly adroop. Languidly, he drew back his shoulder-length mane, now streaked with gray, and slowly allowed the contents of a cold can of Pepsi to wet his 46-year-old whistle.

Soon, however, he would compete in the finals of the Pinch Grand Masters tournament, a new concept designed more for nostalgia than for embattled prestige.

Gonzales has been retired for over a year from the major circuit and, except for playing in 6 of the 11 "Grand Masters" tournaments (winning three), he has spent relatively little time at tennis games. Instead, he has promoted a clothing line and tennis equipment that both bear his name, given lessons at a Las Vegas hotel where he serves as pro, and, like the celebrated Fraser the Sensuous Lion, has dallied at such activities with his wife that Pancho is pappy to a month-old daughter. (He also has had seven other children and a grandson).

With the new languorous life, Gonzales now carries on his 6-foot-3 frame 210 pounds, up 25 pounds from the days he lurked so swiftly, powerfully, gracefully and, yes, viciously on the tennis courts of the world.

In fact, those days are not so long gone, incredibly enough, since only a year ago the regal old lion was still chewing up and spitting out some of the game's better young players—a full quarter of a century after he had first won the U.S. Open title at age 20. Then one day he concluded that his bones ached just too much to go on.

A blue-blazered official now appeared before the reclining Gonzales, and quietly, solicitously began to explain to "Panch" how Gonzales would be ceremoniously introduced to the crowd.

Never moving, Gonzales suddenly broke in. Smiling—one had to take note of Pancho's yellowing but still sharp teeth—Gonzales hissed, "The last thing a player wants to do before a match is talk."

From within those aging pouches, Pancho's brown eyes flashed. His jawbone jumped. The scar on his left cheek glistened. The official recoiled and disappeared in a puff.

"My God," exclaimed a woman in the stands, watching Gonzales now playing Torben Ulrich, "he is still beautiful."

And his passion irrevocable. After hitting his fluid, booming serve Gonzales still attacks the net, only a little less so. His catlike reflexes still permit him to pounce upon nearly every return, only a little less so. And he can still play coyly, only a little more so.

He chanced now to see in the stands the Rumanian Ilie Nastase, a protégé in more ways than one. Nastase, in his late 20s, has hair as long as Gonzales's, but blacker. His temper is as terrible and notorious as Gonzales's. And Pancho has been his mentor and hero. So Nastase, drawn as in a kind of pilgrimage, stops on his way to a match on a nearby court to briefly view Pancho in action.

It is early in the second of a maximum three sets. (It is assumed by directors that the standard five sets is too grueling for "old timers.") Gonzales won the first set but is losing this one.

Pancho smiles at Nastase and points with his racket to a spot on the court. Nastase nods back. Ulrich, the bearded, pony-tailed, finely tuned 46-year-old Dane, serves. Gonzales swats a backhand cross court and out of Ulrich's reach. Nastase laughs and claps and says softly, "Go father."

Gonzales points again, to a different spot. Ulrich watches Gonzales with distaste. One is reminded of how Gonzales, the savage competitor, had always tried to unsettle a rival, using everything down to, as now, a form of disdain. Rod Laver once summed up the feeling of most of the other players toward Gonzales. "He's an absolute jerk," said Laver.

Whack went Gonzales's forehand passing shot. Ulrich lunged and missed. Gonzales looked into the stands and shrugged. Nastase laughed, applauded again. "He's crazy," said Nastase, reverentially. "He always tells me how to hit those shots, and now he tells me again, then shows me. It is like saying, 'If an old man like me can do it, you too can do it, no?' "

Gonzales kept roaring back, sometimes literally, once giving an umpire hell as of yore on a questionable, unfavorable call. The display of enflamed spirit was also instructional for Nastase. Gonzales has told Nastase and others how he came about that unquenchable drive. "I never had the killer instinct until I turned pro and played Jack Kramer on tour in 1949," Gonzales says. "Kramer boiled me in oil. He beat me 17 straight times, unmercifully. And then when I won one he got enraged. It was a lesson in competitiveness for me."

After defeating Ulrich, Gonzales, his long hair now stiff with sweat, said he felt fine but very tired. "Older guys like us don't like to bend much anymore," he said with veteran charm, "and in that second set the ball sometimes got blurry, especially when I went to the net."

Gonzales wiped his dark wrinkled brow with his white

wristband. "Tennis is still fun," he continued, "until the second set. Then it becomes a strain. I know there are two types of tennis, social tennis and competitive tennis. But for me there is just one. When I'm in a match I still don't know any other way than to play to win."

Then the old lion, with gray mane held high, ambled out of the sultry sun. He disappeared into the cool of the covered grandstand where he could loll away the rest of the day, licking his chops.

Henry Aaron: Passive Cobra

Atlanta, August, 1973

First of all, Hank Aaron's swing is all wrong. He hits off his front foot. The great hitting textbook in the sky says you swing with the weight more on your back foot to get—the irony for Aaron—more power.

This is not so bad as when he first played in the Negro Leagues in 1952 and batted cross-handed. That's right, cross-handed; like your Aunt Fanny at the family picnic.

And Hank Aaron looks so passive at the plate, no trace of the cobra he is. "Henry Aaron is the only ballplayer I have ever seen who goes to sleep at the plate," said former big league pitcher Curt Simmons. "But trying to sneak a fast ball past him is like trying to sneak the sunrise past a rooster."

Aaron's nap is a ruse. He has become one of the greatest hitters in history, and is one, two, three or four in runs scored, hits, total bases, runs batted in, extra base hits, home runs and doubles among Ruth, Cobb, Speaker, Musial, Wagner, Mays . . .

Yet he has been buffeted with the faint praise of, of all things, bland consistency. He has been so uniformly outstanding in all areas of play for the last 20 years that, until two years ago when he began to seriously challenge the "legendary" career home-run record of 714 held by Babe Ruth, Aaron was playing in spectacular obscurity.

Aaron had always admired Joe DiMaggio's "cool perfection." But Aaron was cool in the shadows, while DiMaggio was in the glaring cynosure of fame. Aaron is reserved like DiMaggio, smooth like DiMaggio, talented like DiMaggio, versatile like DiMaggio.

But he did not play in New York like DiMaggio. And he is not white like DiMaggio.

Whenever he would hear talk of the greatest players, he was never included. "I'd hear Mays and Mantle and Killebrew and Clemente and Frank Robinson," he says. "I'd never hear me." The lack of recognition rankled.

When professional baseball celebrated its 100th anniversary with a gigantic banquet in a Washington hotel before the 1969 All-Star game, the All-Time team, as selected by writers and broadcasters, was announced. The All-Time "Living" outfield was Williams, DiMaggio and Mays.

"That wasn't so bad," said Aaron, who was on the National League All-Star team that year, "but I wasn't even invited to the dinner."

At the 1970 All-Star game in Cincinnati, Aaron came to the hotel where the baseball headquarters was and asked for a room. He had made a reservation. The clerk checked and checked and said, "Sorry, but we have nothing in your name, we've never heard of you." (This, says Aaron, did not peeve him so much. He has enough perspective of himself to say, "There are a lot of people walkin' the streets who nobody knows.")

"The thing about Hank," says Eddie Mathews, Aaron's one-time teammate with Milwaukee and Atlanta and later his manager, "is that he does everything so effortlessly, so expressionlessly.

"He runs as hard as he has to, for example. His hat doesn't fly off the way Mays's does. Clemente ran, and he looked like he was falling apart at the seams. Pete Rose runs hard everywhere, and he dives head first. Aaron runs with the shaft let out, but you'd never know it. Yet when the smoke clears, he's standing there in the same place as the others."

Aaron has wondered, though, why only recently has he been discovered by the nation. He believes that his blackness was the most important reason. There is a feeling that the white press wants to promote white players. And when one counters that he played in comparatively small towns like Milwaukee and Atlanta, he asks why Johnny Bench is so famous.

Even now he feels sensitive about the diminishment of his achievements. In Atlanta, Babe Ruth chase or no, the team is going poorly and attendance is only slightly more than 11,000 a game.

The letters of racial slurs against his run for the record also, of course, disturb him. And in a lesser way, so do the little slights. Bowie Kuhn, after "warning" pitchers not to groove pitches to Aaron, does not send Henry a congratulatory telegram on hitting No. 700. President Nixon does send a telegram, but he sends it to the Milwaukee Booster Club, of all places. ("Maybe he didn't know my address," said Aaron. He also remembers that President Nixon sent him a Christmas card addressed to "Mr. Frank Aaron.")

An Atlanta paper runs a series on "The Truth about Ruth." One line reads: "While Braves' rightfielder Hank Aaron will probably break Ruth's home run record this year, no one has yet come close to matching the magnetism of the Babe."

Says Aaron, with a grimace: "No BLACK player has yet come close to matching the magnetism . . ."

Besides that, Aaron is now the Braves' "left fielder." He is 39 years old. He was shifted this season from right field because, he admits, "my arm is not what it used to be."

He also knows he is no longer the player he was 10 years ago, "or even five years ago," he said. "It used to be that before a season, I'd know I'd hit over .300, steal 25 bases, bat in 100 runs, score 100 runs and hit over 30 homers. Now I know I will hit over 30 home runs. That's all.

"I'd probably have retired by now if I wasn't going for the record. I'd probably be bored, what with the team 20 games out of first place, and me not able to do all that I once could. I wouldn't want to be an old man hanging on. But this record is so prodigious that I'm going to stay until I break it."

Aaron hit his 714th and 715th homers early in the 1974 season.

Kaline's Questions

Detroit, June, 1969

Night dreamily brooms away day, and through the batting cage mesh you watch Al Kaline, gray tufts in light brown hair behind his right ear, head cocked, reddish neck a light crisscross of lines, bat held high with fingers gripping and ungripping.

His stroke is fluid and the ball cracks away. Kaline runs to first and circles the bases with a soft, deerlike grace, barely disturbing the soil underfoot.

Al Kaline is 34 years old. This is his 17th season in the big leagues. He weighs 185 pounds now, some 15 more than when he came to the Detroit Tigers right out of high school in Baltimore at age 18. Nonetheless, he looks lean and hard-muscled.

This season he is batting around .300 again. He is one of

the few active players with a lifetime average over that mark. He is an expert in his field, as Jonas Salk is in his, Wernher von Braun in his, Picasso in his.

Almost every day from spring to fall, since he was 12, Kaline has hit a baseball, chased a baseball, thrown a baseball.

"Sometimes I wonder what I'm doing, if I've wasted my time all these years," said Kaline, now sitting in the dugout. "And sometimes I think I have.

"I would like to have more to contribute to society. I don't know, maybe a doctor. Something where you really play an important part in people's lives.

"But I never had much education. I had always wanted to be in the big leagues, since I was a kid. And boom—I was there before I knew it.

"Once in a while I'll sit in the dugout and look out on the field and wonder what good is all this, thinking about me, me, me, my batting average, my fielding average. Oh, sure, you care about the team. You have to. But in the end you're worried about you.

"So I have to think of myself as an entertainer, really. Maybe kids can draw an inspiration from what I do. Maybe people who come out to the park can forget their problems for a while by watching me play.

"The difference between ball players and entertainers—actors like Richard Burton or Marlon Brando—is that actors can do different things, comedy, drama, musicals, television, movies. A ballplayer just plays ball.

"But don't get me wrong. A ball game is never a bore to me. Oh, geez, it's great. I love it. Every day there's something new: A ground ball you just beat out, the throw from the outfield to catch a runner, the different situations, the different pitches.

"And for me, as an entertainer, I'd have to be classified as a straight actor. I've always made it on ability alone. No gimmicks. A player like Norm Cash does funny things on the field, talking to fans, catching throws behind his back between innings. It relieves tension for him. I've never needed that kind of outlet.

"I'm there and I do the job. Nothing great. But there is no phase of the game I don't do well. People who know baseball will tell you that. I've never been a one-way player.

"I was a very good outfielder. I'm still a good outfielder, but I don't run as fast as I used to and I don't throw as well. And I used to beat out 12-14 hits a season in the hole at shortstop. Now I'm lucky to beat out one or two a season. But even though I've been a .300 hitter, I don't think I was too much with the bat.

"I was voted by the fans in Detroit on the all-time Tiger team, with the Cobbs and Heilmanns and Cochranes and Greenbergs. Geez, that was some thrill. Like the home run I hit in the World Series in Detroit last year and everyone in the park stood and cheered.

"I feel great so far this season. But the hot weather is coming and that tires me some. I'll play next year for sure. After that, I don't know. I'll sure miss baseball and the people in it. And when I'm done and gone, I think I would like for people to say, 'Al Kaline? He was a real good outfielder.' "

Kaline retired after the 1974 season.

John Carlos's Epilogue

Munich, August, 1972

"What's it been like the last four years? Miserable. I beg here, borrow there, steal here. Hustlin'. When you grow up in a ghetto like Harlem you learn how to hustle," said John Carlos. "Nobody'll hire me. I'm an *untouchable.* All because I took my fist and stuck it in the air.

"Say, what you want, an interview? I need money. I got a wife and two little kids that I been making promises to. Then I show up empty. Come across with some bread, huh?"

Carlos slumped slightly in his chair in the athletic shoe store in the Olympic Village, stroked his beard, stretched out his long legs and agreed tacitly to talk.

Athletes in a rainbow of sweat suits came in to look at shoes, joke and slap palms with Carlos. He is not here as a participant because a short-lived pro football career ended his amateur standing. He is in fact working in the store. He says the shoe company paid his transportation and room here. But that's all. He says he must pick up all other expenses.

He had wanted an executive job with the company, whose shoes he has been wearing and promoting for 10 years ("before other cats ever even heard of 'em"), but says he was refused. "They said I gave 'em a bum image in Mexico City."

In what has been variously described as an heroic, dumb, humanitarian, evil act, John Carlos and Tommie Smith each gave black-gloved Black Power salutes as they received their bronze and gold medals respectively after the 200-meter race in the 1968 Olympics. They were immediately expelled from the Olympic Village there. Carlos said Tommie Smith has had to "hustle," too, until he recently became assistant athletic director at Oberlin College.

Why did Carlos give the salute?

"I tried to do something for mankind," he said. "I wanted to make some kind of statement about the injustices all over the world, not just America. I wanted people to wake up to what's happening in the world. One half the world is rich, the other half is starving. It should be balanced."

Is he involved in any kind of Olympic boycott action here?

"No, and I don't think there will be any from an individual standpoint. The athletes seem younger now and not so socially conscious. I'm not talking about the nation-to-nation thing. That's something else.

"But that's part of the whole political thing about the Olympics. Don Schollander told it straight. He said the Olympics are more political than the presidential elections. You know, why do you have to wear the uniform of your country here. Why do they play national anthems. Why do we have to beat the Russians? Why do the East Germans want to beat the West Germans? Why can't everyone wear the same colors but wear numbers to tell 'em apart? What happened to the Olympic ideal of man against man?"

Has anything concrete come from his action in 1968?

"I think some people, maybe even guys in our government, got their heads together better about some issues like race."

Did he learn anything from the experience?

"I learned that the only difference between America and the other countries is that the other countries are not preachin' this freedom of speech jive. In the States, if they don't dig what you're sayin', you're an outcast.

"I see that 'cause I can't get hired. I got a degree in business from San Jose State. It means nothing. I wanted something in public relations. Nothing. I wanted to make a State Department track tour. They took Bill Toomey, not me. In so many words they told me I was *undesirable*."

Would he do the Black Power salute again if he had it to do over?

"If I felt I had to."

Is he disappointed in not being able to compete here?

"I go down to the track every day and work out. I ran a 10-flat 100 meters the other day. And I see this Russian sprinter, Borzov, who people are talking about. They call him the White Blitz. But that's cool. I'd like to run against him man to man, not black against white. For the competition. But a good white sprinter comes along once every 8, 10 years, like that German a couple years back, and that Italian, and people fuss over 'em.

"Borzov saw me on the track the other night. I was in my sweats. I knew he was wondering if I was eligible."

And the future?

"Maybe I'll be a track coach. I've had offers from Africa. Yeah, I may be forced to leave my own country."

Carlos soon became one of the stars of the pro track circuit.

Boo Morcom at Earth's End

September, 1972

What Richmond "Boo" Morcom did when he finished sixth after being the favorite in the pole vault in the 1948 Olympics was not to crawl deep in to the sawdust pit as he first wanted. Since he was too embarrassed to return home to New Hampshire, he arranged his own post-Olympic tour, visited each foreign athlete who had beaten him, challenged him man to man and topped him.

In the process, he became the first man to vault over 14 feet above the Arctic circle when, wearing two pairs of long johns, he beat the silver-medal-winning Finn. And Boo overcame a problem in Norway when his man was in jail awaiting trial on a drunk-and-disorderly charge. Boo dug into his own pocket, bailed the competitor out, whipped him, and then left for Sweden to knock off the next guy.

Not enough. Boo Morcom, the former track coach and now director of recreation at the University of Pennsylvania, is still beating people. Competition for him is a lifelong fetish.

One would think that at age 51 he long ago traded in his bamboo pole for a hammock. Well, Boo Morcom recently returned from the first World Masters Games in Cologne, Germany, a kind of geriatrics Olympics for about 400 athletes over 40 years of age, held a week after the Munich Games. He won five gold medals, one each in the high jump, the long jump, the pole vault and in two relays.

Not enough. From there he went to Sweden where he set the world record for over-50 athletes in the triple jump, with a bound of 38 feet, 10 inches. He went to London and set a world record for over-50 in the pole vault, with 13 feet 8 inches. A few months before, he had set world records in the over-50 high jump (5 feet 8 inches), the decathlon, the 400-meter high hurdles. He also set the American discus throw record for characters over 50.

He is still a full-haired, strapping Adonis of a physical specimen. He is 5 foot 10 and at 148 weighs only five pounds more than he did in 1948. He says that competition keeps him keen as a shoe spike, physically and mentally.

Rick Owens, a former Penn track man, recalls that practices used to consist of competitions against coach Morcom. "I figured out an event to beat him at . . . the two-handed shotput. You throw the thing backwards, over your head. Boo loved that. On my first throw I slipped, and the shotput went straight up in the air and nearly came down on my head. It landed about a foot away.

" 'Measure it,' Boo said, and then he beat it. I could have been killed. But he won the event."

Boo says he always believed in competition. "And yet they teach technique in sports and not competition," he says. "I always felt I was perfecting myself when trying to beat somebody. Still do." He continues to enjoy balloon-throwing contests or spitting contests ("You wait for just that moment when the wind picks up behind your back") or any other kind of contest or pseudocontest.

He remembers when he was in college at the University of New Hampshire and he would bet his teammates that he could vault well despite obstacles, such as a wheelbarrow placed in the runway (he jumped over it) or 60 chairs put in the runway (he came in at a 45-degree angle) or that he could jump 14 feet (almost an Olympic record in that day) without a warm-up (he would run out from the locker room, be handed a pole and vault). Once he was handed two poles tied together and made that one, too, and refused to ackowledge the trick in order to shake up his fellow bettors.

In the 1948 Olympics Boo was suffering from a bad knee and a wet runway. It had rained for two days before the competition. He had broken the world's record in the pre-Olympic trials and so was still confident. "I was shattered when I came in sixth," he recalls. "Vaulting was my life. I didn't want to go home.

"I got the idea of going into the backyards of the guys who beat me and beating them. It was evil pride combined with a grand passion. Two Americans were first and third, but they knew they were lucky that day and besides I had beaten them many times before. So nothing to prove there."

After beating the Norwegian, the Swede and the Finn, Boo was invited to the house of the Finn, Erkki Kataja, after the Arctic circle triumph.

"By this time," says Boo, "everybody in Europe was calling me the world's champ. I went to this kid's house and met his grandmother. She went to the cupboard and brought out his Olympic silver medal. She asked to see my Olympic medal. She didn't realize I didn't have one. That really put me in my place. I laughed. It showed what kind of bastard I was. But it was beautiful. I could beat him but I couldn't beat that."

Arnold Palmer: Taps?

July, 1968

It seemed more humiliating than lamentable. All sports champions rise, illumine for a day, then sink. Nothing sad in that. But when Arnold Palmer trudged up the bosky fairway toward the 18th hole in the final round of this year's U.S. Open in Rochester, New York, it resembled an unfrocking before a national television audience.

Palmer literally followed the pack. Somehow, he had been placed in the final threesome with amateurs Jim Simons and Jack Lewis.

They trailed the leading pair, Lee Trevino and Bert Yancey. Trevino had understandably leaped in ecstasy after holing out to win. Soon, Palmer emerged on the hilly green. His hair was customarily blowing in the wind. His expression was serious. His "army" was quiet. He was 26 strokes off the pace.

But is Arnold Palmer finished? Was the Open a melodramatic symbol of the eclipse of a great golfer?

A 64-year-old man, the pro since Depression days of the Labrobe, Pennsylvania, Country Club, says no. His name is Deacon Palmer, Arnold's father.

"Don't you believe it," said Palmer senior. "Arnie's still got a good future. He just has to get his putting game going. Nothing wrong with his long game. I was at the Open, and he was hitting as far as Nicklaus and those boys.

"I taught Arnie the grip, the stance, the swing, and a lot of other things. But he's never taken a putting lesson off me. We disagree on technique. He believes in all wrist. I believe in a sweep or stroke, more arm movement. Like Horton Smith and some of the other old boys used.

"Arnold jabs it now. In practice, his stroke is beautiful. But in competition he just doesn't have it. I don't know what's wrong—after all, I've never putted in a national championship."

(At the Open, Palmer said, "My putting was atrocious. I changed grips, stance, you name it. I tried everything but standing on my head.")

Arnold also has problems with his right hip. It began with a pulled muscle in the 1966 New Orleans Open. It is diagnosed as bursae (saclike cavities) in the hip, back, and knee. Arnold has said, "I can do almost anything without being bothered, even running and doing situps. But the violent twisting when I hit the ball does bother me. Complete rest was prescribed. But that's almost impossible for me."

Deacon Palmer played with his son recently. "I noticed it bothered him," he said, "when he wants to pound the ball. I taught him all his life to hit hard, but he can't. It catches up to him. He doesn't finish high like he used to."

Critics have said that Arnold's game would improve if he did not devote so much time to outside business activities. A few years back Deacon said, "Arnold's got to decide whether he wants to play golf or make television films with Bob Hope." Now, Deacon says, "He'd give up anything to win tournaments again. And he will. He's only 38, soon to be 39. He's only a kid. Look at Boros and some of the others. As long as he stays physically fit he'll be around a good while. And he's a clean liver, as clean livers go today."

There is only one major tournament that Palmer, whose pro career began in 1955, has not won. The National PGA. It will be held this year starting July 18 at Pecan Valley Golf Club in San Antonio. His best try was in 1964 when he tied Jack Nicklaus for second place.

"The PGA championship," said Deacon Palmer, "means to Arnold what the U.S. Open means to Sammy Snead. It keeps both from becoming Grand Slam winners. And only, let's see, Sarazen, Hogan, Player and Nicklaus have won the Grand Slam."

Curiously, the PGA has haunted Arnold since boyhood days. In his biography, *Arnie,* author Mark McCormick quotes young Palmer: "All I ever wanted to do was play golf. I would go out by myself and play two or three balls at the same time, one against the other, as if it were a tournament. Sometimes one ball would be me and another one Hogan, and we would play for the PGA championship. . . ."

Palmer went on to win several tournaments, though the PGA has continued to elude him.

Jim Ryun: Gaunt Gladiator

New York, June, 1974

After the last race of the 1974 pro indoor track season, a race in which he ran last, miler Jim Ryun, wheezing like a lean bellows, staggered out of the arena and disappeared into the concrete underbelly below the Madison Square Garden stands.

One wondered if his fading click of cleats played taps for the end of Jim Ryun's poignant career, again.

He had retired in 1971 after having lugged for three years the burden of being considered a loser in the 1968 Olympics, after struggling with hay fever in outdoor tournaments, foul air in indoor tournaments, migraine headaches, the inability to finish races let alone win them. He retired then at the ripe old age of 24, and, soon after, unretired.

Ryun is still the world record holder in the mile, having run his 3:51.1 in 1966. He is at once one of the saddest and one of the most triumphant athletes in American history.

His gaunt face registers pain and little joy. Even in relaxed moments this intense, dedicated athlete seems to gird himself for battle. Perhaps now the bellows had burst, and Ryun would just keep running, on the momentum of his jet stream, to hop his plane and be gone. Track writers remember how, after some losses, he has leaped fences to avoid them, and how at other times they have chugged down a street in pursuit.

But Jim Ryun on this last night of the pro track season was just jogging up and back among the stacked boards from the circus of another day, jogging to snatch back his breath. Then he sat down on a folding chair and answered questions openly from a couple of reporters. Intermittently, he coughed and spit.

"I just couldn't reach down deep when I needed to," he said of his performance. "I just couldn't suck air. Maybe I shouldn't have been here at all, with the migraines and the hayfever I've been suffering from, and all that junk in the air here."

But he is a professional now, one of the big names on the International Track Association tour; he knows he cannot be as aloof as when he was an amateur. And when his name is introduced, he invariably draws the greatest ovation—now he is the "sentimental" favorite.

"I hear the cheers," he said, breathing heavily still, "and they're hard to face up to when you run last.

"You see, I run because I still want to make times, and not strictly for the dollars and cents of it.

"Say, what was my time tonight?"

Someone said, "4:10.9."

"Better than last year in the Garden," he said, with soft smile. "Last year I ran 4:11 flat."

"People ask me how I take defeat," he continued. "I take it like I took victory—in stride. I'll be working in four kids' camps this summer. One thing I'll be telling the kids is that you have to be able to face both."

Ryun, however, like many athletes, takes defeat by not accepting defeat. That is, he can turn a loss into a personal triumph. It is the difference between resilience and despair. Listen:

"In 1968, when I lost to Kip Keino in Mexico City, I still won the race that counted—against the sea-level runners. I ran a 3:37 for 1,500 meters at 7,600 feet. There's not a lot of air up there, you know.

"I never trained at such high altitudes. Kip ran that high all his life.

"But the rest of the country didn't accept that. I didn't expect them to. People were never able to accept me when I started losing. But when you're on the inside you see things other people don't."

In 1972 at Munich, Ryun fell at the start of the 1,500-meter race and was finished.

"It was a victory just to be there," said Ryun. "A lot of people wrote me off, thought I would never even make the team. Then I ran a 3:52.8 mile solo. That surprised a lot of people."

Ryun is even preparing himself not to be let down when his mile record is broken, as he is certain it will be. "I want it to be," he said. "If it isn't, then the sport is stagnating. Nobody wants that. I love the sport too much for that."

He says since he is only 27 years old he has several good years ahead in running. This summer, besides the boys' camps and making some appearances for track such as at the Dewar's Celebrity Tennis Tournament in Las Vegas, he will begin running 20 to 25 miles a day to get in shape for next season.

"I put a great deal of pressure on myself," he said, "but

I've come to realize that if you compete well against yourself, that's half the victory. Looking back on my career, I wouldn't say it's all been frustrating. No, all that pain makes victory—when it comes—all the sweeter."

Bruno Sammartino: "Rassler"

New York, February, 1971

To peer at an ear of Bruno Sammartino is to look upon an object of awesome and grotesque magnificence. The shape is known as "cauliflower," but that renders a sense of the delicate which is altogether what the appendage is not. If the ear were planted, it would be a bulbous potato; if installed, a carburetor. It could also be mistaken for a gnarled fist, a pummeled nose, a mangled big toe.

There appears no place of ingress, as if it were a monolithic rock.

"Nah," said Bruno Sammartino, "it just *looks* like my ears are all plugged. They look ugly from the outside maybe. But there's a little pinhole where sound goes in. What's bad would be if the drums inside were damaged."

How do the drums look? he was asked.

"Worse than the outside," Bruno replied.

"And that's what makes me mad," he added, "all the writers sayin' that rasslin' is fixed and the rasslers are phony and all that garbage. Why don't they go to the state athletic commissions and say, 'Hey, Doc, where does all the blood come from?' It's not ketchup, like a lot of people say it is."

Bruno Sammartino, who had recently lost his World Wide Wrestling Federation Association heavyweight title, gazed into the wash-basin mirror at his long, rugged, and, yes, kindly face that is dominated by unpretentious eyes, an authoritative nose, a prognathous jaw, and those two baleful lugs on each side of his head. Nearby, a deep rumbling swallow of water did not make him flinch.

He had apologized for having to conduct the interview in the toilet room, but the adjacent dressing room area was filled with that evening's combatants, including The Canadian Wolfman, Gorilla Monsoon, midgets Sky Low Low and Little Brutus, and Bruno's opponent this night, Gido Mongol, brother of Bepo Mongol.

"My eyes been gouged, my nose been busted 11 times and fixed twice," said Sammartino into the mirror. "Over this eye I got a scar with 11 stitches, on this cheek 17 stitches, or 18, I can't remember exactly, and altogether I got 67 stitches on my head, but you can't see 'em all because some are on places where I still got some hair left. And my ears—what can I tell ya?"

And all the nights, the howling nights, and all the tasting of resin on canvasses, and the rubbings of ring ropes and all the bristles of armpits that shaped those fearful ears, all this was the result of 15 years as a professional wrestler, the last eight as champion, and all this came into mind now.

And for all the disparagement of pro wrestling as a con game or an exhibition or a farce or a grotesque joke, it still packs 'em in all over the country. The fans are fanatical. Twenty-two thousand of them were on hand in Madison Square Garden this particular night. Five thousand more were turned away.

"It makes me so damn mad," said Bruno. "The garbage they say about rasslin'. But part of it is rasslin's fault. All these guys with gimmicks. My only gimmick is my boots and tights. I'd have some gimmick if I didn't have them, wouldn't I?

"It all started with Gorgeous George, I think. He started with the curls and the perfume and that. You didn't notice the talent before the gimmick. Nobody noticed him when he was just plain George Wagner.

"I've refused to fight guys with gimmicks, and I think the fans appreciate good rasslin'. And we got very loyal fans. Two weeks after I lost the title I rassled in Boston. Fifteen thousand and some plus there. They gave me a standing ovation. I was deeply touched, very deeply touched."

Bruno is proud, he said, of being an athlete, a term not often reserved for professional wrestlers. He said, "I work on weights and techniques three or four hours a day three or four days a week. A sportswriter who is dead now, God rest his soul, said I looked like a squatty, homely, 260-pound guy who was made up of spaghetti and meat balls. That's ridiculous. I don't like to brag, but my appearance is very good. And I've put a lot of training behind my body to get it the way it is now."

At 35, Bruno, born in Italy, is also proud that he has become financially independent, and with only a second-grade education. He said he had his fling as champ and that it was long enough. He is going into semiretirement but will be around for important bouts. "I daresay that if I stay in shape I can rassle to past 40, like Killer Kowalski," said Bruno. "But he's a health fanatic. Terrific vegetarian."

Then Bruno departed to beat the nefarious Gido Mongol. But before that, he rushed into the ring, with an incredible roar of crowd approval (the ecstasy reached Epiphany proportions), to save good-guy Tony Marino, who had been defeated in the previous bout. Mongol had been "kicking" Marino.

"I'm no big hero," said Bruno, afterward. "But if I hadn't jumped in, some fans would've. Oh hell yes."

Someone said to him, in the locker room, that it did not appear as if Mongol had *really* been kicking him in the chest during the bout.

"Did he kick me?" asked Bruno. He sucked in and expanded his huge, highly defined chest. "Feel that! When I flex it I don't give a damn who hits me, I don't feel it."

Jerry West: At Childhood's End

Los Angeles, March, 1974

"If you'd go into an office and see a man my age, a 35-year-old businessman doing some of the things I do with my co-workers, you'd think he was a madman," said Jerry West in the locker room.

"We act like kids, rasslin' and bumping a guy into a door and throwing a ball at him, and the constant riding that goes on in the locker room. You've got to have a lot of kid in you to be an athlete. And, frankly, I've loved it. I feel like I'm the luckiest fella in the world. It's been an incredible life. Incredible. But I don't feel much like a kid anymore. I feel now I should do something more constructive with my life.

"That's why I think that this will be my last season."

Now at the end of his 14th season in the National Basketball Association, Jerry West suits up for Los Angeles Lakers games but sits on the bench. It is a strange and frustrating posture for one of the finest guards—one of the finest players, period—to ever lace on a professional sneaker.

West has played little this season because of a severe groin muscle pull. It causes him pain when he runs, even trots. He can, however, jump. "Yes I could shoot but I couldn't get open," he says, with a wry upturn of his thin lips.

In sports terms, he is now truly "Old Zeke." Old Zeke, the hillbilly from Cabin Creek, with the crooked nose and the nasal twang, was how the Los Angeles Lakers ribbed their West Virginia rookie in 1960. He still has the crooked nose, having broken it eight or nine times, and he still talks as if a clothespin is clipped to his nostrils. But he is a mature Zeke. He is as articulate as an Angeleno, to be sure, and uses none of the hill colloquialisms—he is no West Virginia twig sucker or ridge runner anymore. And he sports a healthy California tan, a far cry from the onetime pale kid and his "West Virginia coloring"—because it is said that there you only see the sunshine at high noon, then it fades over the mountains.

The Lakers, champions two years ago and runners-up last season, have been struggling to make the playoffs this season. The departure of Wilt Chamberlain to San Diego in September took much of the wind out of the Lakers' championship chase. West's injury deflated the team further.

"What hurts so much," said West, "is you don't feel like you're earning your pay." (Which is estimated at $300,000.)

Some of this pain is relieved in places like New York's Madison Square Garden, where West was introduced before the game and received a long, farewell standing ovation not only from the 20,000 fans, but also from the Knicks players, too. West's blue eyes dampened.

He says he is an emotional man; he is also prideful. He says that this will probably be the last time he will ever be in a basketball uniform of any kind. He is not one, he says, to begin playing in YMCA's for the fun of it.

"I've set such high standards for myself that I couldn't enjoy playing the game on any lesser level," he said. "But I'm still very competitive. I'll play golf to satisfy that part of me, and I may go into business or coaching, and I'll set the same high standards for myself in those areas as I did playing basketball."

He says he would like to get away from basketball entirely for a few years; in fact, he'd like to get away from work for a few years.

"I'd like to be on my own for a while," he said. "You know, I've had a coach telling me what to do for the last 24 years of my life." He began his basketball life a skinny kid in Cabin Creek, West Virginia. Later he became an All-American at the University of West Virginia. In 1960 he joined the pros.

"You begin as a kid and you stay a kid in many ways if you are a basketball player," he said. "I took the game very seriously. And the pressures were tremendous. But a lot of the enthusiasm you have to have is childlike. And then you horse around to relieve some of that pressure.

"But I sit on the bench now, and I realize that when you can't do it physically, it changes your mental outlook. You begin to see that you have to do something else with your life. Something more constructive. By that I mean, I want to use my mind. I think I have a good one. I don't want some job where I just sit and do nothing. There's more to me than that, there's more to me than Jerry West, basketball player."

West said that he has been preparing for the end for some time. "I've watched a lot of ballplayers come and go," he said. "And I saw a lot who never thought this athlete's life would end. I didn't want to suffer the kind of crash they did when it was over. And so I think I'm pretty well adjusted in that respect. My ego, my view of myself as a man, was never dependent on how well I played basketball.

"And I've always felt lucky. I don't know why I was never booed. Can you imagine that? Never booed. And I don't know why I've had the success I've had. I mean, take any two guys. They're built alike, look alike, and yet one guy is a better ballplayer than the other. A lot of guys thought about the game as much as I did, had as much desire, and practiced as hard—even harder. I guess someone up there was looking after me.

"And what an indescribable feeling to be cheered. How many men in their lifetimes are applauded the way an athlete is?

"I've enjoyed the camaraderie of teammates. I'll miss that

a lot. But right now I feel like just going somewhere where there is no basketball and there is no coach running my life. But I'll probably miss the hell out of that, too, after about a week."

West retired after a week of training camp the following season.

Hoist the Flag: In Extremis

New York, April 1971

Early this gray April day, the cab driver taking his passenger to the Belmont Park stable area talked about Hoist the Flag. "I saw them pictures in the paper of him on the operating table. Like a regular human being. Anesthetics, surgeons, masks, the works.

"But the bones in them thoroughbreds' legs is like straw, know what I mean? They snap like that. *Every horse that breaks a leg, he's a dead pigeon," said the cabbie.*

Not until the first week in June, about the time the Triple Crown has been run, will it be determined whether Hoist the Flag had won the fight for his life.

"It's about 50-50 right now," said Sid Watters, the horse's trainer. He plucked a blade of hay from the bale hanging alongside Hoist the Flag's stall; the blade drooped from his mouth and he looked at the big, three-year-old bay colt, who now shared the bale with his trainer. "It's getting better each day," said Watters. "We get over one hurdle each day."

On the morning of March 31 Hoist the Flag, just out for a morning breeze, suddenly came up lame. No one will ever know just what did happen. Sid Watters came jogging up the track, ashen. The bone in Hoist the Flag's right hind leg was severely fractured. He underwent a five-hour operation that evening. Hoist the Flag had been the Kentucky Derby favorite and was given a fine chance to become the first Triple Crown winner (Derby, Preakness, Belmont Stakes) since Citation in 1948.

There was a question whether the Derby favorite might indeed be destroyed before the Derby. He will certainly never race again but it is hoped now that he will be saved for stud.

"I'm not bitter," said Watters, "but it was a helluva jolt. Damn, it'll rock you pretty good. Best horse in the world one minute, then you ain't got him the next.

"Nobody knows how good he could've been," Watters said. In the horse's brief career of six starts, Hoist the Flag had never been extended, winning one race by as much as 15 lengths. He won the Champagne easily but was disqualified for interference early in the race.

"It cost us $145,000, but we got over it the next day. It was a jolt, too. But it was only money," said Watters. And two weeks before the accident, money was a factor again. The owners, Mr. and Mrs. Stephen C. Clark, turned down $4 million for their colt.

Hoist the Flag wears a cumbersome cast that covers most of his leg. Only the toe of his hoof is bared at the bottom. He is X-rayed every other day. He is given antibiotics a couple of times a day, his temperature is taken daily, and, of course, he is caressed often.

"But be careful when you pet him," said Watters to a visitor. "He'll bite. He used to have a perfect disposition. But he's smart, smartest horse you ever saw. He knows what it's all about. Besides, he's in agony, and he's got all those doctors around, and needles and shots. Naturally he's going to be irritable. Before, he'd bite in a playful way. But he means it now."

Watters has many fears for Hoist the Flag. It is excruciating for the horse to lie down and then sit up; another crack of his brittle bone would be fatal. Also, there is a possibility of infection or blood clotting or colic. Any one of which would do the horse in.

Watters took the visitor into his office in the barn and showed him a stack of letters on a table. Some had advice, such as putting the horse in a hammock, or tying a big belt around him and hanging it from a ceiling. Others suggested feeding habits: Feed him only oats; don't feed him any oats; feed him only raw natural milk. But all were sympathetic.

"Tell the wonderful Hoist the Flag we are pulling for him," wrote a man in Alabama, "and we know that he will know people love him very much. And he will get well for horses are so much like people. They will try to come back if they are loved."

A Massachusetts minister wrote: "I wish to let you know that in the course of our Palm Sunday sermon we thought of you and your gallant colt."

From a lady in Connecticut: "Whatever happens, please do not destroy him! Would you consider letting him come to Connecticut to recuperate in a beautiful, quiet, natural setting . . . ?"

There was a letter from Wasington, D.C., that Watters somehow missed. When it was mentioned to him, he quickly plucked a pair of spectacles from his shirt pocket.

"There is great hope," the letter said, "when it is recalled that in 1950 Your Host broke his right fore leg. He recovered to sire Kelso in 1960 . . ."

Watters read it over several times. Then he rapped two times on the wooden table.

Hoist the Flag pulled through.

Jackie Stewart Quits

October, 1973

Refreshing to hear of an auto racing driver who retires in one piece, instead of in flames.

Jackie Stewart has walked away from it all, instead of being carried away from it all. He quit a champion, a live champion, an achievement perhaps greater and rarer than all of his record 27 grand prix race wins put together.

He is 34 years old and he figured that he has bucked the odds long enough. Soon they would buck him.

Of course, he doesn't leave his, well, sport, with nothing. He has wealth, memories, and bleeding ulcers. Sunday drives his races weren't.

He admits that his memories helped persuade him that the jig was finally up for him. Several of his best friends were killed in auto crashes, beginning with Jim Clark in 1968.

In 1970, two of his closest driving friends, Jochen Rindt and Piers Courage, lost their lives in races. In early October of this year, Stewart's Tyrell-Ford teammate, Francis Cevert, age 29, was killed during a practice lap for the United States Grand Prix at Watkins Glen, New York. Stewart happened to withdraw from the event, which would have been his 100th grand prix race. One week after Cevert's death, Stewart retired.

Thoughts of death have stalked Stewart.

". . . Somewhere along the line I'm going to make a mistake, whether it be a small mistake or a big one, a mechanical failure beyond my control or someone else's mistake, and then . . ." Stewart wrote those lines in his autobiography, *Faster: A Race Driver's Diary*, published last year (by Farrar, Straus & Giroux).

He remembers talking with Dan Gurney, who had also retired and lived to tell about it. Gurney told Stewart how he lay awake in bed one night and counted all the people he had known who died in racing. "And after a while, maybe an hour, I counted up the number 57," said Gurney.

It seems incredible to someone who sits behind a typewriter for a living—whose only fear is that of being edited—that anyone would want to wash the windows of a skyscraper or drive a race car.

Stewart, though, has been eloquent on the attractions of driving.

"A car," said Stewart, "is very much like a woman, and however banal it sounds, the analogy holds. I know of no better. Cornering is like bringing a woman to a climax.

"The two of you, both you and the car, must work together. You start to enter the area of excitement of that corner, you set up a pace that is right for the car, and after you've told it that it's coming along with you, you guide it through at a rhythm that has by now become natural. Only after you've cleared that corner can you both pleasure in knowing that it's gone well."

Another reason: He said he also continued because he knew that what he did was easier than exposing oneself to the cold, hard workaday world.

Despite the adulation, the action, the romance of the sport, and its tangential advantages, it seems like a game of carburetor roulette. Eventually the whole thing will explode in your face. It is reminiscent of a line from Willard Motley's book, *Knock on Any Door*. The protagonist, a young tough, wished his epitaph to read: "Live fast, die young, and leave a good-looking corpse."

Stewart apparently has lived as fast as he will ever want to. And he neither wants to die young or leave the mortician an easy job.

He also had felt guilty about his wife and children. He says that a racing driver's wife has it harder than her husband. He can escape in the car, "go into the clouds." She must watch and agonize, he said. Waiting for the unspoken inevitable. He did not say that.

And the children. He has two sons. Stewart said that they never understood his work. "Why are you going to drive your racing car, Daddy?" they would ask him. (They have the makings of good, safe, sedentary journalists.)

When he told them he was retiring, he asked them a question: What should I do now?

Paul, age 5, replied, "Write some books and drive our school bus."

Ted Williams and Gale Sayers

September, 1972

Within the space of a couple weeks Ted Williams and Gale Sayers retired. Their departure created a hole in the sports world, a hole about the size of the Grand Canyon.

Williams quit after four years of managing one of the foulest teams in all of baseball history, the Texas Rangers. He said he was going fishing.

Sayers' problem was a bit different. He could run no more. Once the most dazzling, jaw-dropping of runners, he was hobbled by knee injuries. In a preseason game, trying to come back on gimpy legs, he fumbled twice. On the first, the ball was immediately run back into his end zone for a touchdown. The other time the fumble led to an opponent's score.

Chicago Bear coach Abe Gibron, who may be a tactician but not a very tactful one, said that he took Sayers out of the game because he did not want the opposition to score any more touchdowns. This quote buckled the knees of at least one newspaper reader. Sayers quit shortly after and will pursue off-season interests in telecasting and in stock brokerage.

Williams and Sayers are two warm men, besides being two of America's most dynamic sports personalities.

As a player, Williams would waggle his bat with fierce joy and then swat what in baseball parlance is called a frozen rope. As a manager, Williams had problems teaching the young men under him the tenuous delights and theorems of perfection. Those good men Williams did develop, owner Bob Short seemed to trade or sell away. Finally Williams tossed up his arms, saying that his players continued to make high school mistakes.

As a man, Williams is a marvelous entity. He is quick-witted, expansive with anecdotes and, at age 54, convincingly mellow from his sometime sullen days as an athlete.

He did something a couple years ago that will be forever etched in the minds of two newspapermen.

In spring training, manager Williams and a young reporter were sitting alone in the dugout in Pompano Beach. Out of the corner of his eye, Williams saw an old retired newspaperman slowly come down the stairs. "I know him. Damn. What's his name?" Williams said softly, quickly. The young reporter happened to know and whispered it. Williams jumped up, walked over and shook the old guy's hand, calling him by name, asking how he was. The fellow became puffy enough to float into the sky.

In a game, all the crowd and Sayers would watch a kickoff and wait with high expectations as the ball dramatically dropped from the clouds. Then Sayers would take off while the roaring customers and disbelieving would-be tacklers saw him split like a paramecium, in Bill Cosby's words.

"He would throw the right side of his body on one side of the field and the left side of his body kept going down the left side," Cosby once wrote. "And the defensive men didn't know who to catch. They just stood there. Then they looked to the referee for help, because there's got to be a penalty against splitting yourself. But there's not. I looked it up in the rule book and there's no rule against splitting yourself in half."

Sayers, like Williams, is sensitive and discerning. His friendship with Brian Piccolo, which has been hoked up by a movie on the theme, showed this side of him. Piccolo was a white roommate and teammate. When Sayers was presented with the Most Courageous award at a sportswriters dinner in New York in 1970 for his comeback after knee surgery, he said in a moving speech that he was accepting for Brian Piccolo. Three weeks later, Piccolo died of cancer.

At the time of their retirements, both Williams and Sayers had instructional books published on their respective arts and sciences. But for all the charts and graphs and numbered points, the reader can never plumb their magic.

No matter. The unique and wondrous human mysteries of Williams and Sayers have added a good dash of joy to our lives. That's all we need know.

Lance Rentzel and Jim Duncan

New York, November, 1972

When All the Laughter Died in Sorrow is the title of Lance Rentzel's autobiography and could well serve as Jim Duncan's epitaph.

Although Rentzel was a rich white boy from Oklahoma City and Duncan a black boy from a small Southern town, both had much in common. Both were high school football heroes, college all-stars, pros. Both had a certain degree of success and failure. Both lived happily with the first, were shattered by the latter.

Duncan, the former National Football League cornerback, is an apparent suicide at age 26. "Apparent" because not all the facts are known. We know Duncan walked into the police station in his hometown, Lancaster, South Carolina, one late October morning in 1972 and, according to testimony at the inquest, shot himself in the head. The Duncan family, like some other blacks in the South, are suspicious of local police.

What we do know is that Jim Duncan, who felt the soaring joys of being a starter on the Baltimore Colts' 1970 Super Bowl team and being AFC kickoff return leader that season, was terribly depressed from failures during the last year.

He had lost his starting job, was traded to the New Orleans Saints, then was sent to the Miami Dolphins, where he was cut from the squad in September. His marriage of 19 months had broken up; he had suffered a loss of between $22,000 and $58,000 in a wig business; he had a bleeding ulcer and had undergone psychiatric treatment in Lancaster and with the Saints.

"He was afraid of failure," said Harry Hulmes, Saints' vice-president. "And pro football gave him an identity."

After Miami, Duncan no longer had that identity. He returned to a town of 10,000 that had been prideful because of his pro triumphs, to the home of his mother, to no job, to drugs perhaps (he was under police investigation), and to his grave.

Rentzel, now 29, has been a fine wide receiver for eight seasons with Minnesota, Dallas, and currently Los Angeles. His recent history has been highly publicized and notorious. He was convicted in 1966 and in 1970 of indecent exposure.

Each time he was suffering from deep depression. The

similarities to Duncan are striking. In 1970, for example, on the day before he exposed himself to a 10-year-old girl, Rentzel felt that he and the Cowboys were doomed to failure (after losing 39-0). His marriage to entertainer Joey Heatherton was precarious. He had spent almost two years and $25,000 on a "classy" Dallas night club that floundered. He said he couldn't face his friends, family, coaches "or myself in the mirror."

It is all too simple to lay so antisocial an act as Rentzel's exhibitionism on one depressive moment. Rentzel's book, in fact, discussed the story of a man who was not allowed to grow up and who now is finally facing this fact.

He was overly protected by his mother as a child (and adult), sheltered as a gifted athlete, worshiped by fans. "The star performer can't be a normal person," Rentzel writes. There is the sad, insistent striving to prove one's masculinity, thus accepting the "pure drudgery" and virtual sadism of some practice sessions ("They tried to eliminate the softies") and being crushed by defeat.

"The role of defeat or loss is often to play a major part in the appearance of self-exposure as a symptom," writes Dr. Louis Jolyn West, Rentzel's psychiatrist, in the epilogue. "It is as though the patient (nearly always a man) suddenly needs to be certain that his manhood is intact, and is impelled to demonstrate that fact to a female . . .

"And while other elements compounded the problem, his preoccupation with being a winner as a football player (and the tremendous emphasis on winning of the American culture today), was always involved. Needless to say, the tremendous focus of public attention upon star performers like Lance Rentzel, the intense scrutiny given their every move and particularly their mistakes, serves to exaggerate the strain. The pressures by coaches, fans, and the media upon outstanding athletes are almost beyond the comprehension of ordinary citizens."

So we still wonder, are Duncan and Rentzel the only aberrations? Alan Miller, former attorney for the NFL Players Association, told Rentzel: "There are some guys playing in the NFL who've done worse things than you," like taking off their pants and walking bottomless into laundromats, or defecating on automobiles. Dr. West adds that "the need to be brutal or punitive towards one's sexual partner is not uncommon among professional athletes."

Rentzel, after thoughts of suicide, appears to be meeting his problems. He is strong enough to remain in the public eye. And by legal decree he is under constant psychiatric care.

Rentzel writes: "The first thing I had to admit to myself was that I really had an emotional problem. It is only through admitting weakness that one can become strong." One doubts that Duncan ever came to grips with such a realization.

Rentzel, after being suspended from the NFL in 1973 for possession of marijuana, returned to the Rams in 1974.

Beyond the Rainbow

Rainbows and heroes, it appears, are as ephemeral as they are eternal.

Citation: Still a Ladies' Man

Lexington, Kentucky, May, 1969

The spring is gone now in Citation's legs. He walks with much of his former grace and majesty but, increasingly, with more pain. And he seems to need that little extra oomph provided by the slow, easy swing of his sumptuous black tail.

In his paddock, he walks a few yards and stops and lowers his neck and nibbles a fare of grass. His handsome bay coat shines in the warm Kentucky sunlight.

"Ci has got the rheumatism in the legs," said the horse's groom, Hugh Fields, watching and leaning against the white paddock fence at Calumet Farm. "He sets his legs down like a cat with sacks on his feet. That's from an old sayin'—walkin' like a cat with sacks on his feet."

Hugh Fields, a ruddy fellow, tugged his brown cap so it nearly touched his steel-rimmed glasses and he smiled, thinking of Citation. He has been Citation's groom since 1951, when the horse retired from racing after becoming the first thoroughbred to win over $1 million in purses and, in 1948, was the eighth and last Triple Crown winner.

"Ci's 24 years old now," says Hugh Fields. "That's about, oh, 80 years old in human life. He's beginning to break some now—you know, show his age. Got some gray hairs in that black mane, his back is swayed, and he's put on 200-250 pounds since he went into stud. Up to about 1,300 now. He's in top health, though, perfect health I'd call it, 'cept for his legs which been givin' him trouble lately.

"But he's still a ham for posin'. When folks with cameras come 'round, his neck sets up and his ears perk and his back straightens."

For a celebrity of Citation's stature and bankroll, Calumet Farm seems an altogether fitting place to while away the waning days. The cuisine is ripe green (though some say it is tinged with blue). White fences tumble over hills as far as the eye can see. Pink and white dogwood trees are in blossom. Sycamore, pine, and oak trees are slipping into green coats. Jonquils and tulips and red sage and blue ageratum are blooming in the sweet springtime. Here and there, colts and fillies frolic.

Yet it is not all a life of leisure for the famous senior citizen. From February to June each year, Citation must perform daily chores, if they may be termed that. Twice a day during that period Citation the stud is asked to "cover" mares.

"I think Ci's enjoying retirement," said Hugh Fields. "He's still a ladies' man, naturally. He's one of the best covering horses in the country. His stud fee's gone down, though. Three years ago it went from $5,000 to $3,500. Some folks think a horse his age won't get a strong foal. But I don't think so.

"His get never did come up to anything equal to himself. He got some useful horses but not sensational, like Silver Spoon and Guadacanal and Fabius. But you race a horse like the way they raced Ci and they take the stamina outa him.

"But there's no doubt about it that he ain't the greatest horse that ever lived. Would run anywhere anytime on any track. You know what Eddie Arcaro said? He said ridin' Ci was like drivin' a Cadillac.

" 'Bout once a week now he'll gallop 'round the paddock here, but it ain't easy what with the rheumatism in the legs. He likes to roll around, too. Oh, he sure does. Sometimes he'll get mud and dust caked on him an inch deep and it'll take me an hour to clean it off.

"But there'll come a time soon when Ci will lay down and won't be able to get up. He's in perfect health, but he still could die tomorrow. Most horses live only to 18 or 20. 'Course Ci might live to 30, like Man O'War done.

"Bull Lea, that was Ci's daddy, he lived to 29. And a few times a month in those last years he'd lay down and couldn't get up, his legs was so weak. A wrecker would come in with a steel cable and motor and we'd roll Bull Lea onto a girt and hoist him up till he stood and got his senses. Then he'd just walk away.

"Ci still eats good and sleeps good. You can hear him snorin' and groanin' and nickerin' here to Louisville. He's intelligent and level-headed like he used to be. He ain't vicious like some stallions—but he will try to bite you if he don't know you. And he'll listen to you if you talk to him right.

"And sometimes, sometimes when some of us are listening on the radio to a race and the people get to hollerin', Ci will raise up his head and stand straight and listen. He still thinks he's at the track, I reckon."

Citation died one year later.

Jim Parker: Sunday's Woes

September, 1969

Always on Sunday, during the football season, as the clock ticks closer and closer to game time, prodigious Jim Parker breaks out in a rash, welts form around his ears, and his nerve cords begin to quiver like plucked bass fiddle strings.

This pregame physical reaction has been occurring in

Parker for the last 13 years, the first 11 of which were spent in the clubhouse of the Baltimore Colts. The former star offensive guard has been retired for two years now, but he still responds queerly on Sunday afternoons as he stands and fills orders in his package liquor shop in Baltimore.

"I start shaking like a leaf," he says. "Sometimes I think I'm going to get a heart attack. And I get these welts like someone beat me with a stick.

"Something in my body tells me it's game time coming up and I still got this urge to put on a helmet. I can't forget it. This nervousness comes from the mental strain of pro football.

"In the locker room before a game I'd get to thinking real hard about what was going to happen, and I'd get to rocking, from one foot to the other.

"I didn't know what the hell I was doing, and guys have told me that I started knocking tables over and crashing into lockers. Jim Mutscheller, he was an end for us, he used to say that he wouldn't come near me before a game because he was afraid I'd kill."

When games are in Baltimore, the 35-year-old Parker gives his wife and daughter his tickets. He said he just cannot take being there. He never even goes to practice sessions.

"I went once, the first fall I retired," he said. "I was there for 30 minutes to pick up some stuff. I watched some of the scrimmage. But I had to get out of that place fast."

On a Sunday, as it nears 2 P.M., Parker often bounds out of his store, lurches into his car and drives around and around streets in a sort of daze.

"I can't stand still, I gotta move," he says. "I pop these Librium pills in my mouth, nervous pills, been taking them for 11, 10 years, while I'm driving. I don't want to know nothing about what's going on in the game—but I do turn the radio on and off, on the sly to hear what's happening."

He recalls listening in ambush to a recent Colts game

against the Rams and was concerned about how Sam Ball was blocking Los Angeles's rugged defensive end, Deacon Jones.

"I never did have no luck with Jones," said Parker. "I always needed help from Mackey and Curry and the backs. And I was glad I didn't have no part of that Jones anymore."

He remembers feeling sad for one of his ex-teammates, who was called for holding at a crucial moment in the game. And he could picture the reaction of the other Colts. "Eleven years I was holding half the time," he said. "They caught me only sometimes. Sometimes when I did and sometimes when I didn't. But the other players would never bitch at me. Never. But the guys would look at you with a funny look."

One of the hardest things to take now, said Parker, is when the offensive and defensive starting teams are introduced and run onto the field. "I feel like driving my car right onto the field," he said. "But I gotta control myself. I gotta stay away. I tell myself, 'Parker, forget it. It's a young man's game. An old guy like you oughta sit quietly up in the stands.'

"I don't know. Maybe I'll be able to next season."

Joe DiMaggio's Return

New York, February, 1973

Despite Mrs. Robinson's tuneful lament, Joltin' Joe did not leave and go away. Joe DiMaggio returned home to San Francisco because he never really had much stomach for being an American folk hero.

DiMaggio developed an ulcer that can be traced back to his 56-game hitting streak in 1941. (The streak was voted in a poll of baseball stars and executives "the greatest individual achievement in the history of baseball.") The demands made upon him by well-wishers (his word) and business agents forced him to literally bolt his doors and windows.

It drove a shy man even further into himself. He promised himself that when he finished playing baseball he would stay as far away from pressure as possible.

So when he retired after the 1951 season, he slipped out of the public eye. Ever so slightly, however, he has been slipping back.

Recently he showed up in Bowery Savings bank promotions on New York television and in New York newspapers, grayer and balder, and his sad-eyed, long-nosed but distinguished Modigliani face only a little fleshier than when he was the velvet grace of the New York Yankees.

He is also being seen at more pro-am golf tournaments around the country and on rare occasions will attend one of the many banquets that he once always turned down.

He still looks forward to Old-Timers' Day games where the applause for him is longer and louder than for anyone else and where, according to an admiring Reggie Jackson, he still strokes line drives.

"It seems people are still interested in me," said DiMaggio recently. "And some of my friends think that I can do some things in public and not hurt myself, if they're tasteful and if I'm not too pressured."

He said this with characteristic understatement, but also with a *soupçon* of pride and wonderment that a 58-year-old grandfather of two (boys 11 and 9) is still remembered.

Of course, he remembers. Sometimes the memories are pleasantly recalled when he will be watching television and some film shorts of the Yankee Clipper will come on.

Sometimes, though, the memories are literally painful. At the golf tournament here, for example, he came down with a cold. "And I felt all my old baseball injuries come back," he said. (The brim of his blue golf cap was pushed up in front and the eminent DiMaggio took on a Bowery Boys aspect.)

"It seems I had those injuries in every part of my body," he said. "My knee caps got it the worst. I can hardly walk." (Indeed, when he walked down steps he took them with two feet on each step.) "I've got pains in my legs back here and the throbbing from the tendons that I once pulled in my arms. And the ligaments in my shoulders are in shreds. I can't throw 15 feet overhand any more. I've got to throw like this." He made a girlish motion.

He also has quit smoking and he has drastically changed his diet. "I've cut out spaghetti and all those sauces," he said. "I used to eat that stuff a couple times a week."

His schedule for the last 20-plus years has been what he promised himself, one filled with little pressure. He never took any of the managerial offers because "my stomach didn't need it." And even now, when he isn't traveling, he says he is home in San Francisco "doing nothing." Nothing consists of living in the same house he has lived in since his first year in the big leagues, 1936, watching westerns and soap operas on television; he is not very particular of the quality. He reads little except for the sports sections of newspapers and the financial sections, to see how his stocks are doing.

He goes often for relaxing steam baths, and he will spend long hours in his brother's restaurant on the wharf, drinking tea. His ulcer discourages coffee and hard liquor.

DiMaggio blames his ulcer on himself. "I always kept everything inside of me," he said. His former teammate, Phil Rizzuto, has said, "Joe just never blew his top."

Pride in achievement, Joe has said, also caused him inner tension. "Ever since I began playing baseball, I tried too hard. I always wanted to get four hits a game. The first time I came up I'd be worrying about the fourth hit before I even got the first."

He is also terribly meticulous personally. "He keeps promises," said a friend. He remains aware of his physical image. When it was close to tee-off time at the celebrity golf classic, and DiMaggio had not yet appeared, a young athlete asked, "Where's Joe D., combing his hair?"

Even in retirement DiMaggio was conscious of his athletic presence. At first he did not want people to see him play golf for fear his swing was not graceful enough.

And he still will not publicly discuss his short marriage to the late Marilyn Monroe, to whose grave he still sends flowers weekly.

On the surface, it would seem that DiMaggio, in his later years, would go fishing to relax, since fishing was the occupation of his father and his father's father.

In fact, in Ernest Hemingway's *The Old Man and The Sea,* the old man at one point says, "I would like to take the great DiMaggio fishing.

"They say his father was a fisherman. Maybe he was as poor as we are and would understand."

In Al Silverman's unique biography of DiMaggio (*The Golden Year, 1941*, published by Prentice-Hall), Joe says, "It used to make my pop sore when I told him the smell of the boat made me sick. I don't know whether his pride was hurt over the fact that I wasn't a dawn-to-dusk fisherman, like the rest of the family, or because he considered it a disgrace that a DiMaggio should admit to having a weak stomach."

Roger Maris: Bittersweet Memories

Gainesville, Fla., July, 1970

Roger Maris holds a special place in American sports. He performed the unprecedented feat of hitting 61 home runs in a single big-league season and has never been forgiven for it.

To many persons in this quiet college town, Roger Maris is now just another beer salesman. But to many sports fans across the country, Maris is at best an enigma, at worst an object of scorn and, in fact, an iconoclast of sorts.

He retired from baseball two years ago, at the relatively youthful age of 33, and became, with his brother Rudy, the full-time Budweiser beer distributor in Gainesville, Florida, and nearby Ocala. He weighs 225 pounds, about 20 pounds more than he did in 1961 when he broke the revered Babe Ruth's legendary record of 60 homers—which caused Maris as much pain as pleasure.

"If I ever had to have good memories about my baseball career," he said recently, "they probably had to be before 1961."

Few men have had to withstand the withering pressure of publicity that Maris did in 1961 and after, and few men were as ill suited to endure it.

"It would've been a helluva lot more fun to play the game under one mask, and then leave the park wearing another mask. Some guys loved the life of celebrity, like Pepi (Joe Pepitone). Some of 'em would have walked down Fifth Avenue in their Yankee uniforms if they could have. But all it brought me was headaches. You can't eat glamour."

Maris now seems content, relaxed, and happy. His hair is still cropped in a crewcut, his pale eyes are candid and kindly, his dark tie is unfashionably thin, his socks are unfashionably white, his belly is ample and his neck and forearms are still as thick as a slugger's.

"I don't read the papers much," he said, "too busy. Rudy and I drive to the brewery in Jacksonville, we go into the taverns and supermarkets and other outlets to see how our Bud stock is, how it's placed on the shelves. I'm usually out of the house by 8:00 in the morning, and sometimes I don't get home until 1:00 in the morning.

"My customers don't talk baseball much. They used to. But now they'll ask how I think the Cardinals will do or something, but that's all. I never look at the standings. Not at all."

He was asked what he thought of the Yankees' recent winning surge.

"The Yankees?" he asked, smiling. "Did I ever play for the Yankees?" Then, seriously, he asked what division they're in. He did not know.

He has little fond recall for his seven years (1960–66) as a Yankee.

Although he says it is all in the past, "finished and done," his voice betrays a resentment to what he refers to as the "Yankee organization." For one thing, he felt the Yankees did not want him to break Babe Ruth's record. (For much of '61, Maris stayed just a couple of homers ahead of Mickey Mantle as both pursued the ghost of Babe Ruth.)

"They favored Mickey to break it," said Maris. "I was never the fair-haired boy over there. When I'd get hurt, they thought I could still play. When Mickey or Tom Tresh or someone got hurt, they'd let 'em rest.

"I'll never forget the 1965 season. I injured my right hand on about May 18. Ralph Houk, the general manager then, said I should keep trying to play. Finally, with about two weeks left in the season, I went up to his office and told him I wanted permission to go home to take care of my hand, and I said if he didn't give me the O.K., then I'd go anyway.

"Then he said to me, and I'll never forget it, Houk said, 'Rog, I might as well level with you, you need an operation on that.' Now what do you think?"

Maris also felt that many writers did not want him to break the record. "They tried to make me into the mold of Babe Ruth, and I didn't want to fit anyone's mold. I'm Roger Maris. And a lot of the older writers didn't think anyone should break Babe Ruth's record. Some of the younger writers felt they could make a reputation at my expense. So I was called surly. Yet I'd stay and answer their questions, sometimes the same questions as new writers came over to my locker, for two or three hours after a game. If I had that to do all over again, I wouldn't say a word until all the writers were there. Then I'd talk for 15 minutes, and quit."

The controversial and infamous asterisk was placed by then baseball commissioner Ford Frick alongside Roger Maris's name in the record book after the 1961 season. Maris had hit 61 homers in a 162-game schedule, Babe Ruth had hit 60 in a 154-game schedule.

"I didn't make the schedule," Maris said. "And do you know any other records that have been broken since the 162-game schedule that have an asterisk? I don't. Frick should have said that all records made during the new schedule would have an asterisk, and he should have said it before the season—if he should have said it at all. But he decided on the asterisk when I had about 50 homers and it looked like I'd break the record.

"But I understand—and this is only what sportswriters have told me—that when Frick was a New York sportswriter, he was a big drinking buddy of Babe Ruth's.

"But when they say 154 games, which 154 games are they talking about? The first 154, the middle 154, the last 154? If it's the first 154, then I'd still have tied Ruth, because I didn't hit my first homer until the 11th game. If it was the last 154 games or the middle 154, then I'd have broken the record anyway."

If he had it all to do over again, would he have wanted to break the record again?

"I was a professional baseball player," he said, "and when I was out on the field I gave everything I had. No one ever worked harder than me. Baseball was my life then. If there was a record in the way of my doing my best, then the record had to fall. So what's to regret? The fact is, no one ever had as good a season as I did in 1961."

Is there anything he would have done differently during his baseball career?

"Yes," he said. "I would have been more careful not to jeopardize my health. Every day, my body tells me I used to be a baseball player. I can't sleep on my stomach because my rib cage is so tender. It got that way because of how I'd bust up double plays. But that's the way I was taught to play baseball, in the minors, by Jo-Jo White.

"And my knees hurt if I just brush against them. That's from banging into outfield walls. And I still don't have any feel in the ring finger and little finger of my right hand, from when I broke my hand in '65."

Maris announced plans to retire from baseball after the 1966 season. Then the Yankees traded him to the St. Louis Cardinals. He played two more years for them. (It was Cardinal owner August Busch who helped establish Maris in his present business.)

"With the Yankees," said Maris, "I was booed for 81 games at home, and for 81 games on the road. You say it doesn't affect you, but it does, finally. All that stopped when I went to the National League. Oh, I got booed the first series at Shea Stadium against the Mets, but the booing stopped after then.

"I knew it would be different in St. Louis on Opening Day in '67. The team was paraded around the field in open convertibles. My name was announced and the people cheered. After those seven years in New York, I felt that, hell, there is some good left around here yet."

But no longer was he a long-ball pull-hitter, because of his injured hand. "I couldn't tell anyone because then the pitchers would know—and they found out soon enough. But I became a guy who tried to punch the ball over the third baseman's head.

"Finally, I couldn't stand to play any more. I'd had my fill of it. The game itself was enjoyable, but the traveling was the big factor. It's not the kind of life for a family man . . . It's all in what you like."

Maris now has six children, ranging in age from 4 to 12. Roger Jr., 11, and Kevin, 9, play in the local Little League. "I haven't encouraged them to play, and I haven't stopped them," he said. "They haven't asked for my help, and so I haven't done nothin' with either one. Better they play the way they want to."

Would he want to return to baseball as a coach or manager?

"I don't say I'd *never* want to, but right now I like it down here in this small town, and I'll let the other guys do it up there. It's fun to sit back and watch.

"You know, but I was happy my first year in New York, in 1960, before the writers stuck the poison pen up my tail. But now, when I think about the good times, I think that I was just as happy my first game in the big leagues, in 1957 with Cleveland, as I ever was.

"I remember we played the White Sox, and Billy Pierce was pitching against us. They beat us 2-1, I think. But I got most of our hits. I went three-for-five. We only got five hits altogether.

"I remember that a couple days later I got my first major league homer, up in Detroit. It was with the bases loaded. I don't think many guys can say that their first big-league homer was with the bases loaded. But don't print that, it might sound like bragging.

"But the 61 homers? I don't think much about that. It's in the past. And I'm too busy now, anyway. Maybe it'll become important to me when I'm 65 or 70. Maybe then I'll think about it, and enjoy it."

Joe Nuxhall: Youngest Big-Leaguer

Cincinnati, Ohio, October, 1972

On opening day of the 1972 World Series, before 51,726 empty seats that echoed with the crack of a bat, and behind the protective screen at the mound, a capless and baldish and heavy-bellied 44-year-old ex-big-leaguer, sweating in the morning sun, smoothly threw batting practice to the Cincinnati Reds, and let his fancy fly.

"Sure, I'm filling up the stands in my head," said Joe Nuxhall later. "And I'm wishing I was 10 years younger. I never played in a World Series. Every guy who's ever put on a baseball uniform dreams of playing in one."

He spoke hoarsely. The Reds' radio announcer (and regular batting practice pitcher) since he retired as a player in 1967, Nuxhall said he had strained his voice with "war whoops" on the air during the Reds' last-game, last-inning winning rally against the Pirates in the play-offs. "I like announcing, it makes me feel I'm still a part of the team," he said.

"But I'd still love to be pitching in the Series. It seems I've always been a little too early and a little too late."

Nuxhall, a sweetheart of trivia fans, began his big-league pitching career on Saturday, June 10, 1944, at age 15 years, 10 months and 11 days. It was during the war of course and there was a drought of good baseball players. Nuxhall was a precocious 6-foot-3, 195-pound, left-handed junior high school and sandlot star in Hamilton, Ohio, 25 miles north of Cincinnati. The Reds signed him. When he was called in to pitch on that June day, he became the youngest man-boy ever to play in the major leagues.

"People always ask me about it," he said. "But I never get bored telling it. I'm proud to have been signed, to know people thought I was good enough.

"But if I knew then what I know now, I wouldn't have done it. It took away a lot of things. Actually, they wanted to sign me when I was 14, but we had a good junior high school basketball team and I wanted to stay on it for another year.

"If I had waited until my senior year in high school, I could have signed for a big bonus. Bonuses were starting then. Hugh Radcliffe was the first, I think. He signed with the Yankees. He got about $50,000. I got $500 and a salary of $175 a week." He shook his head.

"Also I might have gone to college and got myself a good education. I miss that."

Nuxhall had been coming down to Cincinnati and sitting on the Reds' bench every day after school in that 1944 season. "I never expected to play," he said, "and I'd just shag flies in the outfield before games. But I was happy, especially since I hadn't seen many big-league games before. So it was a thrill to just sit on the bench and watch."

Then one day manager Bill McKechnie called Nuxhall in the dugout. "I heard him, but I didn't believe he was calling me," said Nuxhall. "He had to call twice. He sent me to the bullpen. I threw the ball all over hell. I went into the game in the eighth inning. We were losing 13-1. I was shaking all over. I was going to face the Cardinals, Stan Musial and his troops."

He got the first batter on a grounder to short, walked the next, made the third pop out to short, walked the fourth, the fifth singled, the next three walked and the ninth singled. Now it was 18-1.

McKechnie came out and said delicately, "I think you've had enough for today, son."

Nuxhall did get two batters out, and he says it took him eight years to get his third out in the major leagues, to lower his 67.50 earned run average.

He threw temper tantrums and wild pitches in the minor leagues in 1945, then voluntarily retired (you can look it up) in 1946 and got his amateur standing back to play high school baseball, basketball, and football in 1946–47. "I got lonely for high school sports," he said.

After high school, he returned to the Reds' organization and floated around the minors until 1952, when he came up again to the big leagues. He had some good seasons, like 17 wins in 1955 and also played in the All-Star game that year. But by 1960 he was being booed "every time I turned up." And he was traded to Kansas City the next season, which was the only season that he did not play for the Reds and, agonizingly, the only season they won a pennant during his playing career.

He returned to the Reds in 1962 and was now, inexplicably, being cheered. He finished his career with a respectable record of 135 wins, 117 losses.

His dubious record of having been the youngest major-league player will probably stand forever, since rules do not permit teams to sign a player until his high school class graduates. But he smilingly doubts that he might become the oldest, too.

"Even though I might be able to pitch an inning in a game now, or even in five years, it might be too dangerous," he said. "My reflexes are a little slower and I've already got hit with line drives a couple times in batting practice because I wasn't all the way behind the screen. Once Pete Rose hit me in the kidneys."

He laughed. "But sometimes, yeah, I still live a little bit of it in my head, pitching again in a game, in the World Series."

Casey Stengel the Vaudevillian

New York, February, 1974

"Even though Babe Ruth ran me out of vaudeville," said Casey Stengel, "I still can't knock him."

"Now this fellow in Atlanta is amazing. He hits the ball the best for a man of his size. But I can't say he hits the ball better than Ruth. Ruth could hit the ball so far nobody could field it. And that's even with the medicinal improvements today. They come along now with the aluminum cup and it improves players who only used to wear a belt and it's better for catching ground balls."

Stengel jumped up on his bowed, lumpy but still spunky 84-year-old legs and hounded down an imaginary ground ball that bounded under the coffee table.

"I got an offer from Van and Skank, the biggest names in vaudeville—they were from Brooklyn—to go on the stage after the 1923 World Series.

"I hit two home runs to win two games in that Series. I hit one in the first game and one in the third game. And this was when I was with the Giants and the Yankees were already the Yankees with Babe Ruth.

"Now, I remember Ruth when he was a young pitcher with the Red Sox. I batted against him, and this was before he grew the barrel on his belly but he always had those skinny legs. Well, they figured they could make more money with him in the lineup every day instead of every fourth day so they moved him first to first base but they had a good fella there so they moved him to outfield.

"In that series I hit an inside-the-park homer to win the first game. I was 33 years old. And I had a bad heel so I wore a cup in my shoe. The cup started comin' out when I was roundin' the bases. All the pictures show me like this"—head with hunk of white hair thrust back—"and like this"—head flung forward, rheumy blue eyes wide, tongue thrust out from his deeply stratified face—"and puffin'."

"So then the vaudeville guys asked me, could I sing. Sure I can sing"—for his voice sounds like cracked stained glass—"and can I dance? Sure. They wanted to pay me a thousand dollars for a week. And I wasn't making but five thousand—maybe six thousand—for a season playing ball.

"I was riding high. But the Yankees and Ruth said, 'Better watch out,' after I got the home run. It was a threat to brush me back. In the third game I hit a homer over the fence to win the game. And I ran around the bases and I made like a bee or a fly had got on the end of my nose and was bothering me. I kept rubbing it with my thumb, and sticking my five fingers in the direction of the Yankee bench . . . Commissioner Landis fined me for that.

"So I began to practice my dancing and I thought I'd be the new Fred Astaire. But then Ruth hit three home runs in the last game and the Yankees won the Series and vaudeville forgot about me and nobody heard from me again for 10 years.

"So now Ruth, he could have gone on vaudeville. Hell, he could have gone to Europe. It was near the end of my career and pretty soon I commenced managing. Ruth kept on hitting homers. Aaron is going to break his record, and so the National Broadcasting people asked me to talk for three minutes about Aaron being better than Ruth. I couldn't say that.

"It's a livelier ball today, and Aaron was up more times. And they use the fake fields, and the balls whoosh through faster. But Aaron is amazing the way he can hit 'em with his wrists.

"Now, Ruth struck out a lot. But any damn fool knows that nobody pays to see the world's greatest singles hitter. Or the world's greatest doubles hitter. Ruth was the world's greatest home run hitter and that's what everybody wanted. And that's what he gave 'em.

"It worked out okay for me, too. Because I'm still in baseball—vice president of the New York Mets ball club and in the Hall of Fame—and who knows what my future in vaudeville would have been. Just like I started out to be a dentist. The dean of my school said, 'Why don't you be an orthodontist?' That way I could have got a lot of rich kids and put a black filling in their mouth.

"The dean said, 'Always try to be a little different.' And today I make speeches all over. People ask me, Casey, how can you speak so much when you don't talk English too good? Well, I've been invited to Europe and I say, they don't speak English over there too good, either.

"So, you can see why I can't knock Babe Ruth, even though he drove me out of the vaudeville business, can't you?"

Pete Gray: One-Armed Brownie

August, 1971

What is Pete Gray doing today?

"Don't do nothin' but play a lot of golf," he said by telephone from a tavern in Nanticoke, Pennsylvania. "I shoot in the 80s, usually. Once shot 79."

Pete Gray plays golf left-handed. That is, with the left hand only. Just as he played outfield, hitting .218, with the St. Louis Browns in 1945. He lost his right arm when he was six years old. He is 54.

"Just got out of the hospital," he said, speaking rather loud as if unaccustomed to phones. "Ulcers. Used to drink pretty heavy. Lost weekends, that kind of thing. But I don't drink any more.

"Say, could ya hold on for a minute. I got a cigarette here, I wanna take a couple puffs of it."

The phone banged and dangled against the wall. Gray does not have a phone in the 12-room house where he lives with his mother and brother. You can reach him by calling the tavern down the block. If he's not playing golf, he'll answer the phone, sometimes.

He says he doesn't have a home phone because people would be callin' all the time. Like the Hall of Fame in Cooperstown. According to a local man, the Hall of Fame has been trying to get Gray's glove for its collection. "But Pete says the glove is somewhere in his cellar and he'd just as soon let it rot there," the man said.

"Hello," says Gray, "back on."

He says he weighs about 145 pounds now ("pretty thin") after the ulcer operation, about the same as he weighed during his one big-league year.

"People always ask me, how did I throw," he said. "Well it's impossible to describe. The way I done it was all in one motion. I'd catch the ball and stick the glove under the stub of my right arm."

And hitting? "When I was a kid I'd go up to the railroad tracks in town and take a stick and throw up a rock and hit it for hours and hours. My father was always mad because I was late for supper. Developed a pretty good wrist, though."

The year before he came up to the Browns, he played for Memphis, stole 65 bases and was named the Most Valuable Player in the American Association. These were the war years and the caliber of professional baseball was at low ebb. But in 1945—or any year, for that matter—for a one-armed man to play 77 major-league games and bat .218 and hit six doubles, two triples, drive in 13 runs and strike out only 11 times in 234 at-bats is quite a feat.

"I packed 'em in all over," recalls Gray. "There were 65,000 in Cleveland the first time I played, and I hit a triple my first time up. When we played the Yankees the first time in New York, our team was introduced before the game. Luke Sewell was our manager. He said, 'Pete, you stay here, be the last one to come out on the field.' I got a standing ovation—just to make an appearance! But I done a pretty good job, too."

Gray lost his arm when he fell off the running board of a huckster's wagon and his arm caught in the spokes of a wheel. Soon, however, he was playing baseball in the streets of Nanticoke, a coal mining town of 20,000 persons, six miles from Wilkes-Barre.

"By the time I was 16 I was better than the other kids," he said. He came to New York in 1939 for the World's Fair, and took his glove along because he had read that there were big-league tryouts in Brooklyn. He eventually caught on in the Canadian-American League, and in his first game dived for a fly ball and broke his collar bone. He wound up hitting .381. The next season he moved up to Toronto where he got a late start; he had come down with the grippe.

After 1945, he bounced around the minors—Toledo, Elmira, Dallas—haggling over contracts and having drinking problems. In 1950 he played for the House of David club, and two years later got a call to play in an outlaw league in Canada.

"And that was it," said Gray.

He says that except for baseball he has never worked a day in his life, though an old *Sporting News* clipping said that he had left the Dallas team to return to the billiard parlor he owned in Nanticoke.

A local woman says that Gray doesn't seem to have much money, but doesn't seem to care about it either. He plays golf almost every day, she said, and she thinks his buddies pick up the tab.

"And Pete refuses to go on public assistance," said a man who works in the Nanticoke post office.

Gray was asked what he lives on.

"Nothin', never done no work," he said. But what do you use for money?

"Well, I saved some from baseball," he said, reluctantly. "I did a lotta gamblin'. My mother she rents six rooms in the house and she gets a check because my father died of black-lung from the mines, you know."

Gray says he's a celebrity in town. "Wouldn't you think so?" he said. Though he seems proud of his baseball career, he hardly seems to revel in it.

"It's done," he said. "They don't run the railroad here any more. It's all weeds where I used to hit the rocks. And the ball fields I played on, they're all woods. Time changes."

Could there ever be another one-armed big-leaguer?

"I don't know," he said. "I see that some high-school kids been playing with one arm. But you gotta put a lot of time in, like I done."

All About Moe

February, 1975

While reading *Moe Berg: Athlete, Scholar, Spy*, I was reminded of a line from Dylan Thomas: "I like very much people telling me about their childhood, but they'll have to be quick or else I'll be telling them about mine."

I like very much people telling me Moe Berg stories, but they'll have to be quick or else I'll be telling them mine.

The co-authors of Moe's biography, Louis Kaufman, Barbara Fitzgerald, and Tom Sewell, aren't quick enough.

In good time, they tell us about how Moe went from the Princeton campus to the big leagues (turning down a Romance language professorship at Princeton to do so), how Moe was fluent in 12 languages, how Moe became a lawyer during off-season studying at Columbia, how Moe inspired the famous appraisal, "Good field, no hit," how Moe infiltrated behind enemy lines to learn and evaluate Nazi scientific secrets.

They tell us how Moe filled his rooms with worldwide newspapers and wouldn't allow anyone to sit on the chairs because the newspapers, he admonished with a smile, "were alive." And we learn how Moe took three showers a day, was briefly the enormous star of the popular radio quiz show, "Information Please," and how he was the warm friend of people from Ted Williams to Albert Einstein.

"I kept looking at this man," Ted recalled about his rookie year. "He must have been about thirty-six or so and I was just a kid. And I kept saying to myself, 'Is this Berg guy some kind of an act, or what?' I watched him and watched him, listened to him, and his special uniqueness never faded. I concluded it wasn't an act but here was a special kind of different human being. . . . He was something to remember and he certainly had a real man's guts."

The book relates an anecdote concerning Albert Einstein. And here particularly I wanted to insert my two cents' worth. The story goes that Moe was visiting Einstein's home at Princeton. Berg had written a story for the *Atlantic Monthly* magazine entitled "Pitchers and Catchers." Einstein in the same issue had written about the atomic bomb.

Einstein, it is recalled in the book, said, "I read your story in the magazine, Mr. Berg. You teach me to catch, and I'll teach you mathematics."

There is a punchline that Moe added when he told me the

story. Einstein went on to say, "But let's forget about it, because I'm sure you'd learn mathematics faster than I'd learn baseball." And then the pair went back to sipping the tea Einstein had made, talking, and then listening to the professor play his violin.

Moe told me about this in one of the numerous talks we shared in a variety of baseball press boxes, until his death at age 70, on May 30, 1972.

He was a tall, lean, darkly complexioned man with neat, wavy, gray-black hair in his later years. He always wore a black suit, black tie, black shoes, white shirt. He was a man widely open to new thoughts, new people, new joys. And he was very, very secretive.

When I once asked him if he had ever written anything, he said, "Only a treatise on Sanskrit." Not true. I later discovered the *Atlantic* piece, published in 1941. When I mentioned it, he said, with some delight about my detective work, "You caught me." And he never, never discussed his secret work during and after World War II.

Moe's father, a Ukrainian-Jewish immigrant, never approved of his brilliant son's ballplaying. Neither did Moe's brother, Sam, a Newark physician. Dr. Sam once told me, "Moe could have been a brilliant barrister, but he gave it all up for baseball. And all baseball ever gave him was his happiness."

Moe was decidedly happy at baseball games. He enjoyed the company of young sportswriters, particularly, I believe, because they (at least I) were enthralled. Unlike, I may add, the young ballplayers. Moe once told me that he would never go down into the dugouts like some oldtimers.

"Once when I was with Boston," Moe said, "Roger Peckinpaugh, a great shortstop in his day, visited our dugout. I remember Williams whispering to me, 'Who's that old geezer?' 'Old geezer!' I said. 'He was a better hitter than you'll ever be.' It wasn't true, but I thought I'd just shake Ted up a bit, give him some historical perspective.' "

In the press box, Moe would like to point out what pitch would be forthcoming, why a second baseman just missed getting his glove on a grounder ("The team arrived late last night and was up early this morning—not enough sleep").

I sat behind Moe during the opening game of the 1971 World Series in Baltimore. He sat next to Jimmy Cannon, the fine, doughty, veteran sportswriter, who also had a penchant for discussion. But during the first several innings, Cannon was quiet. Berg talked. Moe would turn to ask me and some of the other young sportswriters what we would do in this and this situation.

Periodically, Moe recalled how he had blocked the plate in 1928 in a similar circumstance against Ty Cobb, how he had called this pitch in this predicament for Walter Johnson. For most of us, it simply added a beautiful patina to the game. But Cannon, wearing a cap, stared straight ahead, unspeaking.

Near the end of the game, Moe asked again generally what we thought might now happen in this crucial situation. Cannon could take it no longer. He muttered from under his cap, "If you'd be quiet for a minute we'd find out."

Howard Kitt: A Never-Was

June, 1972

Howard Kitt never made it to the major leagues, which may have been the best thing to ever happen to him.

In the fall of 1960, at age 18, he was signed off the Long Island sandlots by the New York Yankees for a figure in excess of $60,000, still one of the highest bonuses ever tendered by the Yanks.

He was a left-handed pitcher who struck out hitters with

mechanical frequency. He can still recall headlines, "Strikeout Whiz Kitt," and he can still remember all those laudatory words, like Yankee manager Ralph Houk's, in Florida spring training of 1961, saying that Kitt's name comes to mind first when he thinks of his hard throwers.

"And you know, one pitcher in that camp was named Ryne Duren," says Kitt.

The Yankees were the Bronx Bombers in those days, and Kitt intellectually reasoned that he had little chance of sticking with the big-league team.

"*However,*" he says today, "I romanticized that Whitey Ford was getting older and the Yanks would be needing a left-hander soon. It might not be *me,* but then again, why not?" And he dreamed of another headline: "Young Phenom Makes Club."

It wasn't to be. In the next five years, the 6-foot-3, 190-pounder would pitch for Modesto, Amarillo, Greensboro, Richmond, Augusta, Columbus (Ga.), Binghamton. He would develop bursitis in his arm and lose the fast ball that Ken Harrelson, at Modesto in 1961, said was even faster than another pitcher in that league, Sam McDowell.

Howard Kitt had also been a good student. In off-season he studied economics at Hofstra University and eventually graduated cum laude. After his fifth season in professional baseball, he decided that he was stagnating, having dropped from Triple A ball to Double A.

He recalled some of the guys he had played with along the way, who "had mud thrown in their faces" yet stuck in the minors despite being released from one team and hanging on by fingernails with another.

Columbia University offered Kitt a fellowship in economics in 1965 and he accepted. He gave up baseball and his big-league dreams. He is now a thesis away from a Ph.D., has taught economics at Hofstra and is currently a consultant for the prestigious New York consulting firm of National Economic Research Associates.

He is aware, of course, of some of the pro ball players—the "Boys of Summer"—who struggle in retirement, having known little but baseball all their lives.

"Maybe that would have happened to me, too, if I had gone on to the major leagues," says Kitt. "I don't know. But since my career was kind of shaky, I began to read more widely and began to become more introspective. I was no longer single-minded about baseball."

His interest in the game now, at age 30, is still high. He watches games with, he says, "a jock mentality."

"I love the center field television camera," he says. "I work on the hitter with the pitcher."

He goes to games infrequently but when he does go, there is a mixture of pain and nostalgia.

"For instance, when I watch Mel Stottlemyre, I picture myself in a Yankee unie. I played with Mel in Modesto and Greensboro, and we roomed together in Richmond. I see Mel running sprints in the outfield, and I think, that could be me with him, since Mel and I ran sprints together a hundred times."

Yet Kitt refuses to dwell on these thoughts. What's past is not prologue for him. He has not pitched competitively since 1965, when he was 12-3 with Binghamton.

"I was asked to pitch on several Industrial League teams, but refused," he says. "I want people to remember me as a hard-thrower, not some old slob pitching Sundays for some semi-pro club. And I don't want to be cannon fodder for some young guys coming up who want to make a reputation." But Kitt cannot help feeling fortunate in the way things have turned out.

Last season, Baltimore pitcher Tom Dukes, an old minor league friend, was in town and called Kitt to get together.

"I was happy to, but I felt some trepidation," recalls Kitt. "We shared a lot of dugouts and laundromats, a lot of hopes, and a lot of problems, and I wondered if Tom would want to talk about those minor league days.

"He did, because it was a happy time, a time when the world was all before us. Now, Tom's curve—in economic terms—is going down. And mine—well, I think I'm on the way up, in my business. He is concerned about what he'll be doing after baseball. And since then I've thought about Curt Blefary, another guy I played with, who has just quit baseball. Curt said he'll become a cop. And I see Roger Repoz—we broke in together—described as a 'veteran outfielder.' In my mind's eye, Roger will always be a 23-year-old kid playing at Modesto where actual gophers came out of holes in the outfield.

"But when Tom Dukes said good-bye last year, he said, 'Howie, there's no way in the world you shouldn't have been pitching in the big leagues.'

"And for a moment, that got my juices flowing again."

Jackie Robinson: Hope by Example

November, 1972

Days after Jackie Robinson's death, I was still thinking of a lunch I had with him about four years ago. I had walked into his midtown Manhattan office to pick him up. He was on the phone, legs up on his desk, talking to some friend about a celebrity golf event to which, this year, he had not been invited. Robinson had gone to several previous tournaments in the series.

He wanted the friend to find out why there was no invitation. Did it have anything to do with some of his recent controversial remarks about "racism in America." "We'll give it a good fight," Robinson said, smiling. He had the shaft of his glasses in his teeth.

Jackie Robinson, it seemed to me, *enjoyed* the fight. Even

then, at age 49, suffering from diabetes, failing eyesight that would render him virtually blind before his death, high blood pressure, heart trouble, and the drug addiction of his son, Jackie, Jr., he was still combative.

"Look at Jackie now," wrinkled Satchel Paige told me a couple years ago, "and his hair's white and you'd think he was my grandfather."

He didn't sound old, though speaking in that dynamic falsetto he sounded more like Liberace than you'd expect of this rough ex-ballplayer, who was so menacing on the bases, who suffered so many pitchers trying to stuff baseballs in his ear, who broke the color barrier in a white elitist game and had to live with "black bastard" echoing through the dugouts and the caverns of his mind.

At Jackie's funeral, however, the Rev. Jesse Jackson's eulogy rang through the great vaulted Riverside Church, and the phrase for Jackie Robinson had changed from "black bastard" to "black knight."

Robinson had become a Hall of Famer, but his place in history does not stop at Cooperstown. Baseball provided the setting for a milestone in the American human rights struggle. Robinson helped open the doors of opportunity not only in sports but also in many other areas of America.

Jesse Jackson compared Robinson to Louis Pasteur and Gandhi and Martin Luther King and Jesus, as a man who gave others hope by example. This may seem a wild exaggeration. But if you were a 13-year-old black boy like Ed Charles living in Florida—where blacks were still being lynched—it was not so wild.

"I owe so much to Jackie Robinson," said Charles, an ex-major-league infielder. "All black players do. We tend to forget. I never will. When Jackie Robinson came through my home town with the Dodgers in 1947, it was the biggest day of my life. It was the biggest day of all our lives.

"I realized then I could play in the major leagues. They

pushed the old people to the ballpark in wheelchairs and some came on crutches and a few blind people were led to the park.

"When it was over, we chased the Dodger train as far as we could with Robinson waving to us from the back. We ran until we couldn't hear the sound any more. We were exhausted but we were never so happy."

I told Robinson at lunch that day that I had recently been in Chicago and had talked casually with a black shoeshine boy in his early teens. I asked who his favorite baseball player was.

"Ernie Banks," the bootblack said. "Willie Mays, too. Yeah, I wanna be a ball player, too. Like him."

I asked the fellow if he wanted to be a ball player like Jackie Robinson, too?

"Who?" he asked. "Never heard of him."

This was neither sad nor surprising to Robinson. He dealt in realities.

"It's true that many black kids have never heard of me," he said. "But they haven't heard of the Montgomery bus boycott in 1956, either. And that was the beginning of Dr. King's nonviolent movement. They don't get any kind of black history in their school books. They want it. They read only about white society. They're made to feel like nonpersons. This is frustrating. It's up to the power structure of this country to understand these kids. Then the burnings, the muggings, the dope, the despair, much of what plagues this country will be greatly lessened.

"Black athletes playing today carry prestige. They can be very significant in explaining the problems and encouraging the kids. But I've been out of baseball for 12 years. The kids look at me like I'm just an old-timer."

The "old-timer" fought until he died. He fought for better housing, he fought for better schooling, he fought for greater say for blacks in government, he fought for a black manager in baseball.

While he angered the mossbacks who thought he wanted too much too fast, he continued to inspire others with the courage of his fight that would encompass freedom for all men.

"No grave can hold his body down," said Jesse Jackson, "it belongs to the ages. His spirit is perpetual. And we are all better because a man with a mission passed our way."

Carmine Vingo: Rocky's Victim

New York, January, 1971

There was no heat in the large office building on Broadway, and Carmine Vingo, a big man in blue uniform, stood in the tomblike marble lobby and rubbed his rough, chilled hands together. The midnight cold crept under the glass-door entrance. Carmine Vingo shivered and uttered a quiet oath that ended in a puff of breath.

"Cold," he said. "I ain't got no radio tonight, neither. The guy with the radio busted his back and he's in the hospital. His room is locked with the radio in it."

Carmine Vingo is the security porter here ("People say security guard, but it's really security porter"), and on this wintry Sunday night he would have to keep one purblind eye on the door while he mopped the floor, emptied the ashtrays, scrubbed the elevators.

"Who'd ever believe it?" Vingo asked. "I figured the worst that could happen was to get knocked out. Actually, I was figurin' on winnin'."

Vingo was referring to another wintry night, December 30, 1949, the day after his 20th birthday and a few weeks before he had planned to be married. He fought Rocky Marciano. It was the first 10-round event at Madison Square Garden for both. Vingo had a 16-1 record and he and Rocky and Roland LaStarza were considered the best young heavyweights around and one of them, said experts, would surely become champion.

Vingo was knocked out in the sixth round; he did not get up. He did not regain consciousness for three weeks. He was paralyzed for two years, his right leg is still stiff, and he is partially blind in both eyes.

"I can't drive a car no more, I can't walk so good no more. I can't even put my pants on without leaning against the wall. Imagine that! And I can't dance no more. Used to love to do the Lindy Hop," said Vingo.

He speaks softly, hoarsely. His salt-and-pepper hair is combed carefully back in stiff lines. His face is clean-shaven but bluish from a heavy beard and a trace of pock marks. His eyes are soft brown and lingering. His nose is flat. He appears older than 41.

"There were two other 10-round fights after us that night," said Vingo. "Both guys who lost, Ruben Jones and Dick Wagner, used to live in my neighborhood in the Bronx. They'd come by and visit and they blamed *me* for their losses. 'Carmine,' they said, 'we were slippin' in the ring because all the water they threw on you.' "

A few months after he left the hospital Carmine Vingo married his sweetheart, Cathy. They moved in with her folks.

"And all the neighbors thought we were rich because of all the rumors that we were collecting thousands from all over the place," said Vingo. "What a laugh. The only money we got was from Cathy working. I couldn't hardly get out of bed for two years."

There were and are no pension plans for prize fighters (though recently there has been a slow movement in this direction in New York). "Pension?" said Vingo. "They didn't even have a stretcher. I heard that six guys carried me out of the ring."

Another belief was that Rocky Marciano was helping Vingo financially. In fact, after Marciano died in a plane crash on August 31, 1969, the New York *Times* obituary read: "Despite his reputation for conservative spending, Marciano had a list of beneficiaries to whom he sent money regularly. One of these was Carmine Vingo . . ."

("The only thing we ever got from Rocky were promises," said Cathy Vingo recently. "He'd tell Carmine that he'd have something going for him soon, to put him in some business, that he had some property for him in Florida, that he'd have a benefit for him. Nothing. Each man is for himself in the fight game. That's the game.")

"I didn't care," said Carmine, blowing on his hands in the lobby. "But my wife gets mad about it. I didn't push Rocky or Al Weill, his manager. Maybe if I'da pushed . . . But I'm not the type. Rocky, he was one of the nicest guys you'd ever want to talk to. I'd go up to his training camp in the mountains. And I was at his wedding and met his family, wonderful people, his aunts and cousins and uncles. And I went to his funeral. Paid my own way. My wife came in one morning and said, 'Carmine, I got terrible news. The radio said Rocky Marciano was killed in a plane crash.'

"I never asked Rocky for nothin'. But he did send me two tickets for his second fight in Chicago with Jersey Joe Walcott. Sent two round-trip plane tickets, too. And you know, I never did get my purse for my fight with Rocky. It was $1,500. It went for doctor bills. I had four private nurses, and the whole bill was about $4,000. I still don't know who paid that. It coulda been Rocky. But he only got $1,500, too. And he couldn't have had much money because he was just startin' out, just like me. He didn't start makin' it big 'till after our fight."

Carmine makes $125 a week now and things are getting tougher. The house of his in-laws, where he has lived for 21 years, is being torn down by the city for a housing project. He must find a new apartment. He needs three bedrooms because he has a son 12 and a daughter 10.

("I don't know where we're going to move," said Cathy Vingo. "We pay my parents $40 a month now. Rents everywhere are so high. Everything's over $100 a month. And this is a new job for Carmine. He worked in Jersey for 15 years, but he had to quit because carfare was too much. To cross the bridge one way was 55 cents.")

Carmine Vingo shrugs. "We ain't rich and we ain't poor but it's not so easy either," he said. "I think about what happened, and I got to shake my head. Twenty years old. I was 20 years old and my career was finished. That wasn't all. A couple months later I was in a school yard watching a softball game and a guy swings and throws his bat. Guess who it hits in the nose. *Carmine.*"

He smiled and blew on his hands again.

Joe Louis: Black King

"Outside in the villainously lit streets—they still have gaslight in darktown Baltimore in 1937—it was like Christmas Eve in darkest Africa. This, it turned out, was the night Joe Louis won the heavyweight championship, and for one night, in all the lurid darktowns of America, the black man was king."

—from One Man's America, by Alistair Cooke

Rochester, N.Y., February, 1970—It had begun two years before that night, Joe Louis was saying, in the same month, coincidentally—May, 1935—when he knocked out Primo

Carnera, and Jesse Owens, a sophomore at Ohio State, broke three world track records and tied a fourth.

"The colored people back then could raise their head a little bit finally, 'cause their head was hung low for a long time. And they walked a little straighter up, 'cause their backs was bent low for so long," said Louis.

Louis recalled this in his dreamy way as he slouched in a chair in a hotel room here in Rochester, New York. He was famous for that slouch, and his shuffle, and his serene demeanor, and his pithy comments despite a lack of education, and for his swift fist that knocked you over like a train roaring out of a tunnel.

The sun came through the window silently and highlighted the pores on his tawny, heavy face. And some of the tight curls of his hair showed white. He is 55 years old and had won the championship nearly a third of a century ago. Yet, as one 27-year-old black man said when he saw Louis recently, he is still an idol and a symbol of the heights a black man can reach in America, and the man said he still goes through the scrapbook of Joe Louis that his grandmother gave him when he was a boy.

Louis was in Rochester for the Hickok Belt Athlete of the Year banquet, and would receive the "Golden Links" award as a sports hero of the past. He said he felt like Jack Dempsey did a few years back at this same banquet, that he did not know how the people would accept him because he was "out of the past." As it turned out, like Dempsey, he received a standing ovation.

Louis was the second black man to hold the heavyweight title. Jack Johnson, was the first, early in the century. But Johnson was an iconoclast and was generally unpopular among blacks as well as whites. "Johnson might have set the colored man back some," said Louis.

"I think I just come along at a time when white people began to know that colored people wouldn't be terrorized no more," he said. "Many of them had been terrorized through the land and was what they called Uncle Tom's people. And the Ku Klux Klan came into being and colored people were scared to move hardly.

"When there was one colored man in a town who wanted to get ahead, maybe get a little better house than the next man, there'd be some other colored fella and slip 'round to tell the whites. 'So-so tryin' to make it big.'

"So I came along, and Jesse, and now the colored man had somethin' to look forward to. And the way I carried myself during that comin' up made some whites begin to look at colored people different.

"I kept my nose clean, and I acted like a gentleman, like an American."

Jackie Robinson has said that he felt Branch Rickey admired Joe Louis's comportment so much, it inspired him to sign Robinson as the first black man in organized baseball.

"I never knew Branch Rickey," Louis went on, "and I didn't know that about Jackie and him that way. But I knew Jackie from the Army, we was at Fort Riley together in 1943. I helped get him his officer's commission. Fort Riley was not the liberalist army camp, and they didn't let no Negroes go to officers' school. When I found out, I called someone I knew at the Secretary of War office in Washington. There was a big investigation, and Jackie and a lot of the others went to officers' school. I paid for a lot of their officers' uniforms. The army doesn't give you officers' clothing. And most of the colored men was too poor. I didn't buy Jackie's. He had money.

"Jackie is my hero. He don't bite his tongue for nothing. I just don't have the guts, you might call it, to say what he says. And don't talk as good either, that's for sure. But he talks the way he feels. He call a spade a spade. You need a lot of different types of people to make the world better. But I never felt insulted about prejudice. I felt sorry for them.

"I think Paul Robeson did more for the Negroes than anyone else, even though someone like King did a lot. Robeson went to Russia in '36 and he said this place is better for the Negro than in America, more opportunity, better treatment. What happened was the American politician got mad and said it was a lie. Ralph Bunche is a result of that. They gave him a chance after that."

Louis went on to say that "Cassius Clay could've done more for the black man than I did. But he missed his opportunity. He could go into places now. He could count now. He should have belonged to the people, not to just one segment of the group." He referred to the so-called Black Muslims. And it was shameful, said Louis, that South Africa denied Arthur Ashe a visa. "Sports should never be involved in politics," he said.

Louis was asked, as he flipped open the top of a can of orange soda with his very large hands, what he feels his role in American history is, and has been.

"I was in sports, and it is sports that has done more than anything else for race relationship all over the world, not just America," he said. "I was in Germany not too long ago. I wanted to see East Germany. Well they told me how sourpuss the Russians were. So me and a few others went to Checkpoint Charlie.

"A man on the other side recognized me and wanted to take my picture. This Russian soldier comes over and says no picture. The man told him who I was. The Russian soldier throws his arm around my shoulder and he says, 'Take my picture, take my picture, too.' "

Jake LaMotta: Philosopher-Bouncer

New York, November, 1973

Inside this darkly glittering, rock-pulsating, many-mirrored topless emporium, a supple blonde, one of five shimmying maidens, ends her choreographic stint. She steps down from the bar stage and walks past the nearby tables. She wears a G-string with bills—tips from admirers—tucked like green butterflies down her rear side.

"Kiss, honey, gimme a kiss," urges Jake LaMotta, from behind his cigar. She smiles, decorously kisses the hefty ex-middleweight boxing champion on the bridge of his well-worn schnoz and departs.

"A nice broad," said LaMotta, who is the keeper of the peace, so to speak, here in mid-Manhattan. "But she's young. She don't know nothin' about life or love. It's true, yout' is wasted on the young—that's not my original saying, it's someone else's.

"But me, I'm 50 years old, and I gone through two million bucks, four wives, 4,000 pounds, millions of punches and been with—you won't believe this—a thousand women, at least.

"I made all that money goin' up and comin' down from being the champ, and I always had a weight problem so I had to lose a lot of pounds. And the women, well, a friend of mine once told me that they like me 'cause I'm the ultimate in manhood.

"I always been symonymous (sic)—is that how you pronounce it?—with beautiful women. But the next time I get married—I been divorced now from my number four ex for a year—I'm goin' to marry a woman uglier than me. So far, I ain't found one that fits the description." LaMotta laughed.

"And I know I ain't gonna find her here. Funny thing, I love women but I'm turned off here. You seen one topless broad, you seen 'em all. I don't mean I'm like a faggot—it's more like a gynecologist."

Another employee in microscopic frock walked by and sat briefly on LaMotta's lap upon request. When she left, LaMotta was asked why he shows the ladies so much attention if they don't titillate him.

"Showmanship," he replied. LaMotta prides himself on being a sometime after-dinner speaker, maker of television commercials and actor in a couple of Hollywood movies (one being called, fittingly, *Cauliflower Cupids*).

"What would make me happy is a woman I can love. I need a relationship. I need a woman I can communicate with.

"Happy. Who the frig is happy? So many negative things throughout the universe. Sure, there's sunshine, but there's storms and hurricanes and blizzards and floods. We got to get rid of our negative feelings and become spiritual.

"That's why I became a Christian Scientist eight years ago. Matter does not exist. The *soul* exists. That's what they believe. You have to almost hypnotize yourself. Like rain and winter don't exist for me. I don't own no winter coat and I don't own no rain coat.

"Whatever the mind can conceive and believe, the mind can achieve. That's not my quote, either, but it's right. Think about it. See that ash tray on that table? If you believe strong enough you can make it move. "He stared hard as a bullfrog at the small black ashtray. It seemed not to budge. "Unfortunately," said LaMotta, "I haven't reached that level of consciousness yet.

"The Law of Karma has the right attitude about life. You only get out of it what you put into it. Like jealousy. I used to be a jealous guy with my broads. No more. Life is too short. Jealousy is a disease, a negative thing. It's all wrong.

"My life now, it's a period I'm goin' through. I been a bouncer here for almost two years. I accept it. I don't feel sorry for myself. Don't forget I been in jail, in a chain gang, was put in a box in a hole in the ground. And I been punched silly. So this place is not terrible. I do my job. They don't want me to sit in a window and advertise myself the way Jack Dempsey does in his restaurant down the street. Because here, they ain't sellin' me, they're sellin' tits."

He has plans, though. "There's negotiations for a movie on my autobiography, *The Raging Bull.* I'm in a vending machine business with my brother. And I got my public speaking and acting. Nature provides, makes your skin tough. If it don't, you end up in the looney bin.

"I learned to have patience. Ride with the punches. I did plenty of that! And I was always good at self-hypnosis. I wanted to be champ, wanted to be champ. Dreamed it, wished it, believed it. It came true."

He excused himself for a moment to shoo away some teenagers who were peeking through the door of the window-covered bar.

He returned and spoke of the after-effects of a boxing career. "All those punches I took in the head must be why I talk kind of funny," he said. "But I don't know. I didn't talk so good when I started, either." He discoursed briefly on world affairs: "The only honest politicians are them guys who ain't been caught, and they're hypocrites."

"I amaze myself," LaMotta continued, puffing languorously on his cigar. "I've become a philosopher in my own right. Say, you got a lot of good information from me, don't ya?

"Maybe you could write the article from the standpoint of

a philosopher ex-fighter. People think fighters are stupid, punchy—and most are. But we got good hearts."

Jack Dempsey: Peachy Caveman

New York, February, 1970

"If Joe Frazier bites me, I'll take one back outta him," said Jimmy Ellis, laughing and showing large, white teeth. "Johnny Morris bit me in Pittsburgh a couple years ago, and I just bent over and got my chunk from him."

This testimony on carnivorous delights was delivered one afternoon in a dressing room in Madison Square Garden as Ellis, his fluff of reddish-brown hair bent over while he laced a boxing shoe, prepared to work out. On February 16 he would meet Joe Frazier at the Garden to decide the heavyweight championship of the world.

The discussion began when a sparring partner asked Ellis who it was that gnawed Rudell Stith that time. Ellis said it was Randy Sandy. Angelo Dundee, Ellis' trainer, recalled that Oscar Bonzvena once savored Lee Carr's neck. And Teddy Brenner, Garden matchmaker, remembered when Terry Young mistook Paddy DeMarco's shoulder for a fillet.

They were still laughing about it when Ellis came up to the workout area. He was grabbed immediately by photographers, who already had apprehended a gray-haired, dark-suited, dignified gentleman named Jack Dempsey.

Mr. Dempsey did not look much heavier than his fighting weight of 180. His hazel eyes were a trifle rheumy, but maybe that was from the glare of his red sweater.

"Glad to meet you, Mr. Dempsey," said Ellis.

Very polite, very nice young man, Mr. Dempsey would

later say of Ellis. And Ellis would say, "From all I've heard and from all I've read, Mr. Dempsey was some hard man."

"It's much, much different nowadays," said Mr. Dempsey, taking a seat at ringside to watch Ellis spar. He looked around at the crowd of 200 or so. "When I went to training camp, like at Luther's, upstate in Saratoga, there'd be 2,000 people up there. It was jammed. And very nice. The air was beautiful, water was fine, and good swimming too."

Ellis was introduced and so was his first sparmate, Rufus Prassell. Mr. Dempsey placed his cigar in his mouth and clapped politely, like milady at the opera sticking the lorgnette in her eye and applauding softly.

"Sure," Mr. Dempsey replied to a question, "some people still call me champ. I was champ for six years, 1919 to 1926—that's seven years, isn't it? That's long enough. But they're nice people. You know, 'Hiya champ, hiya champ.' Still makes me feel good."

The bell rang, and Mr. Dempsey gave the sparring his full attention. Both fighters wore red gloves and stern expressions.

Earlier, Mr. Dempsey had watched Frazier spar. He said, "A rough, tough fighter. The kind of fella who's on top of you all the time."

The former champion noted that Ellis was more on the boxing type, and that he moves pretty good and throws 'em pretty fast.

Mr. Dempsey was asked how he would fight Joe Frazier, who has a crouching style. "Gotta get the man up," said Mr. Dempsey. He did not raise his right arm off the arm rest, but he made a quick fist and gave an upward snap of his wrist.

Though he is 74, there was an electricity of brute power in that gesture, and it is easy to see why a reporter in the 1920s was shocked when he came to Mr. Dempsey's room the morning after a title fight and saw Mr. Dempsey, this man-eater, in silk pajamas.

Someone asked who he was picking. "Let the best man win," Dempsey said, civilly and with a kindly grin. "I don't want to make any enemies."

After three rounds, Mr. Dempsey rose to depart. He said good-bye to Ellis and to the other fight people. On the way out he shook the hand of his old friend Lester Bromberg, boxing writer for the New York *Post*. Then Mr. Dempsey lifted Bromberg's hand and bit it. Just like that.

"Caveman," said Bromberg later. "He's always been that way. A peach of a guy."

Joe Frazier knocked out Ellis in seven rounds.

Jim Thorpe and the "Scoop"

February, 1973

It was not widely known that Roy Ruggles Johnson wrote what often is considered the greatest sports "scoop" of the first half of the 20th century. But the impact was worldwide and tragic and is still in the news.

Obituaries across the country carried the fact that Johnson, who died at age 89, wrote the story disclosing Jim Thorpe's professionalism.

Johnson was the county editor of the Worcester (Mass.) *Telegram*, when he wrote the copyrighted story that broke on January 22, 1913. He was tipped off that a man visiting relatives nearby was bragging that he managed Jim Thorpe on the Rocky Mount, North Carolina, baseball team in the Piedmont League. Johnson found the manager, who told him that Thorpe, an outfielder, had been paid $15 a week.

Johnson returned to his office, flipped through his Reach Baseball Guide and saw Thorpe posing with a smile in the Rocky Mount team picture.

The story resulted in the Amateur Athletic Union stripping Thorpe of medals and trophies he had won in the 1912 Stockholm Olympics (where he had won, incredibly, both the decathlon and the pentathlon).

Thorpe tried to explain: "I did not play for the money. I was not very wise to the ways of the world and did not realize this was wrong. I hope I will be partly excused by the fact I was simply an Indian schoolboy and did not know I was doing wrong, because I was doing what many other college men had done, except they did not use their own names."

His medals were never returned and his name has not been restored in the Olympic record book despite various efforts through the years. Today, a group headed by former Yankee pitcher Allie Reynolds, also an Oklahoma Indian, plans to petition the President to plead the case to the International Olympic Committee. Don Johnson, son of Roy Ruggles Johnson, says that his father supported the idea that Thorpe's name and medals be restored.

"My father felt that the AAU was too strict," said Don Johnson, now an executive with the Worcester *Telegram.* "There were other athletes playing for money under assumed names in those days, and Thorpe was simply guileless to that."

Did Roy Ruggles Johnson ever regret writing that story?

"I'm sure he didn't," said Johnson. "The old gent—that's what my brother and I called my father—was a man of rectitude and high moral principle. He felt it was his job as a newspaperman to write the story.

"He never boasted about the scoop. He rarely talked about it. In fact, I didn't know he had written it until I was in college.

"And he never exploited it. He never wrote magazine stories about it. A year after the story broke he did get a job with the *Boston Globe*, but he didn't even get a writing job. He got a desk job, and I'm sure it had nothing to do with the Thorpe story."

It was the lone scoop in Johnson's life. He went on to write some 3,000 columns for the *Globe* on Yankee folklore. Meanwhile, he followed Thorpe's career, which went from pro football and major league baseball to drunkenness, destitution, three marriages, and, finally, death in an obscure trailer at age 64.

Johnson, himself a teetotaler, continued to believe in the sanctity of the free press, according to his son.

"It was the classic example of a dedicated newspaperman doing his job," said Don Johnson. "It takes a lot of integrity to tell the truth when the truth is unpalatable, as it so often is.

"I was always glad about one thing for my father. That was what happened when he met Thorpe in 1952, forty years after the Stockholm Olympics. The *Boston Globe* sponsored a Sportsmen's Show. Thorpe came, since he was a great fly-caster. Someone got the idea to bring him up to the office to meet my father. They had never been face-to-face before.

"My father said, 'Jim, I'm proud to shake your hand. I always thought you were the greatest athlete that ever lived.' Thorpe bore no rancor to my father. 'You were only doing your job,' said Thorpe."

Thorpe died one year later.

In Washington, Grace Thorpe, a daughter of Jim's, said, "No, I don't think the loss of the medals or the fact that his name was taken off the record books made much difference to Dad. He felt that his achievements were proof enough of his abilities.

"But I would like to get the medals back to put in the Indian Hall of Fame in Kansas. And I'd like Dad's name restored in the official books. It would be for Indian kids, something for them to try to emulate."

Johnny Weismuller: From Pools to Jungles

New York, November, 1972

"If I had my advice to give Mark Spitz," said Johnny Weissmuller, running a hand through his long orangy hair, "it would be to get humble, to come back down to earth."

Weissmuller recalled a moment at Munich when he sat in the stands with Spitz's parents. Spitz's mother held a bunch of flowers. Spitz had just won one of his seven Olympic gold medals.

"He walked by just below us and I called, 'Hey Mark, your mother's got flowers for you.' He didn't even turn around. That's the kind of kid he is, I guess. I don't know, maybe he hypnotizes himself."

Weissmuller, at a restaurant to receive an award as one of the 50 top athletes of all time—undefeated for 10 years, winner of five Olympic swimming gold medals in the 1924 and 1928 Olympics—said he understood, however, how a guy can get cocky.

"But I got it knocked out of me pretty quick," he said. "It was early in my career, and I had already set a bunch of world records. This one race, it was a 200-meter free style, I walked past each opponent as they lined up and whispered, 'Where you going to finish, second? third? fourth?' My coach, Bill Bachrach, he wanted to know what I had said. I told him. He ordered me to go back and apologize to each one of those guys. I did. But I was so mad I won the race by 10 yards."

Weissmuller talked about a recent magazine article, "The Selling of Spitz," which said Mark Spitz is being marketed by businessmen who do not allow Spitz or his family to speak to reporters or business associates about Mark's life.

"Isn't it awful," said Weissmuller, scrunching up his nose. "But I guess you do have to be careful about business. I was never very good at it. I'm a good guy. People used to say sign here, and I signed.

"My first agent in Hollywood got me into trouble. He cost me half a million. I'm still trying to sort that mess out with the Internal Revenue Service. And it's been years."

Weissmuller says he is now semiretired, but remains active in promoting Johnny Weissmuller swimming pools and is director of the Swimming Hall of Fame in Fort Lauderdale, Florida.

He is nearly 70 years old ("68," he corrects, "70 sounds so old") and says he still swims about two hours a day three days a week. "I just fool around in the water," he said. "But a year ago I jumped in for the hell of it and broke a minute for 100 meters. I did it in 59.4 seconds. No one my age can do that. So I'm still a champ."

He laughed, as he does often, his front teeth slightly touching his lower lip. Although his hair is dyed and his face has an easy sag, he still carries his weight well over his 6-foot-4 frame. He says he weighs about 210, some 20 pounds over his competitive weight.

A white silk kerchief was knotted around his thick but somewhat wattled neck, and an undershirt peeked up from under the salmon-colored shirt that covered his still huge chest.

"I've had some ups and downs," he said, "but it's been a ball. I didn't have much formal education but I went around the world six times. I've had five wives and each experience was like going to college."

He also had some trouble with alcohol—"bloody Marys

are still my soup"—but he can still let out a savage jungle yell "when I'm full of beer."

His high-pitched jungle yell may be his most famous single possession now. For 19 years he was Tarzan, of the Apes and of the movies. By 1947 he had literally outgrown his Tarzan loincloth. And for the next 10 years he stayed fully clothed as Jungle Jim.

He went into the swimming pool business after that. But he says he still gets letters from all over the world: "Egypt, Russia, Africa—they want pictures—and they send it to Johnny Weissmuller, U.S.A., and I get them at my home in Titusville, Florida. Amazing, isn't it?"

"Kids still see those Tarzan movies," he continued. "I've got seven grandchildren. Half of 'em don't believe I'm Tarzan. We see one of my movies on television, and I'll say, 'That's me.' And they'll say, 'Oh no, that's not you, grandpa.' "

He chuckled and repeated, "It's been a ball. I was a kid from Chicago who was too poor to own swimming trunks until I was 12. But I've spent a million dollars, and I'll spend another million before I'm through. And, you know, I was fortunate to be a swimmer. That's one sport you can do forever. You can be a hundred years old and wheel yourself to the pool and fall in. And the older you get the warmer the water becomes—I mean, it feels better.

"Swimming clears your lungs out, too, makes you able to yell louder." He let out a sort of subdued yell, which turned only a few heads in the restaurant. He chuckled.

Not long after, a waitress came by, asked Weissmuller for his autograph. He pulled out a preautographed postcardlike photograph of him swimming. He carries a batch of them inside his sport jacket pocket for just such occasions, which, he says, are numerous.

The waitress recalled that she had seen Weissmuller do comic diving at the 1939 World's Fair in New York.

"When you get a certain age," she said, "all you have is memories."

"Make some more, honey," said Weissmuller, with a naughty but nice wink.

Gisela Mauermayer: Nazi Star

Munich, August, 1972

Skeletons of enormous crocodile heads lie in glass cases and greet the startled visitor as he enters the drab lobby of the Munich Zoological Institute. It is here also that another relic, a one-time proud and powerful sports symbol of Nazi Germany, works as a librarian.

Gisela Mauermayer is now 58 years old; she walks tall, though without starchiness, looks fit, smiles with pleasant blue eyes. Yet in her lined face is the weariness of her life since World War II.

Recently, in a downtown theater, she saw herself in a film about the 1936 Berlin Olympic Games. She saw herself, a mighty six-foot Aryan beauty, win the women's discus throw and better the Olympic record by an amazing 23 feet. She saw herself on the victory stand give the stiff Nazi salute as the swastika flag was raised and her national anthem played. The stadium crowd of 100,000, including Adolf Hitler, boomed with cheers.

She remembers that chilling experience as the proudest moment of her life.

"I felt I had lived up to a responsibility to my country," she said, now, sitting in a white smock at her desk. "I was very nervous before the event. I was the favorite. I felt that if I would lose I would be disgraced in the eyes of Germany."

She and her schoolteacher father "were very enthusiastic

about the Nazi movement." And the pressures were great for her to live up to the glorious tradition of Teutonic superiority in mind and body, as trumpeted by the Nazis then.

"I was very patriotic," she said. "Germany had lost the first World War. And for a long time we had foreign occupation. Hitler was the man who had driven them out. Millions joined the Nazi party. My father and I joined not for profit but out of idealism. Years later it was not possible to get out of the party. But I saw that the Nazis were doing evil to people who could not defend themselves—beating them in the streets—like the Jews and others who did not have leanings toward the Nazis."

By 1938, she says, she refused to join a Nazi teachers organization. She said she never gained anything by being in the party, and her only promotion as a physical education teacher in Munich during the war came because she had been an Olympic gold medal winner.

When the American forces entered Munich, they robbed her home of her athletic trophies and her gold medal. She and her father were kicked out of their teaching positions because of their Nazi affiliation.

"I tried next to regain my life," she said. She first got a job "as a simple worker" planting vegetables in a garden. Later, she made little dolls' houses and sold them herself. In 1947 she was summoned to a postwar trial, with many others.

"It was to classify us as strong Nazis or weak Nazis," she said, with a dry smile. "I was classified a weak Nazi. I was fined 200 marks and then I was given a—how do you say—white waist coat?"

She apologized for her halting English and thumbed through an English-German dictionary on her desk. Then she said brightly: "a clean slate."

She was allowed to enter the University of Munich, where she received a doctor's degree by studying the longevity of bees. In 1954 she became librarian of the Zoological Institute.

She lives now in the same row house in Munich as she did before the war. She is a spinster and lives with her sister. She has a piano and cello in the living room and plays chamber music often. Every year, she says, she goes skiing for a fortnight. She teaches a class in gymnastics once a week. For the last two years she has been taking yoga classes. "It is relaxing, and the movements are calm—better for you after you reach the age of 50," she said.

For a time in the 1950s she was active with the female committee of the German Olympic Committee but has dropped it because she feels the idealism of sport is fading.

"I do not envy today's athlete," she said. "They work too much. They have little freedom for personal purposes. They are like machines. They have special doctors and take chemical substances for increasing their strength."

Despite the emphasis on sport in her time, she says her life was still "more free and careless" than it is for the athletes of today.

Her interest in sport is still great. She was thrilled to be a guest of the German Olympic Committee at the 1972 games. But she was not impressed by the multi-million-dollar Olympic Village. "It is too grand," she said. "It is really a town, very narrow, and the dormitories are nearly skyscrapers. In 1936, I remember that the Olympic Village was really a village. It was 20 kilometers from Berlin, and it was bucolic. There were little cottages in the woods for the athletes, and lakes and trees and flowers all around."

She recalls that it was a good time for the athletes, and those involved were not very much aware of the propagandizing and the military displays and jackboots clicking through the streets. "I was not so conscious of Hitler and his crew," she said, "until I won the gold medal and we shook hands in a back room a half hour later. He said to me, 'Wonderful performance.' It was exciting."

Fraulein Mauermayer attended the 1952 games in Helsinki as the supervisor for a group of high school scholars from

Germany, and she says that was the only Olympics she has known about in which there were "no politics, only pure sport."

She said that the 1956 Melbourne games, 1960 Rome games and the 1964 Tokyo games were all designed mostly to gain money for those cities. The 1948 London games refused on political grounds to allow athletes from the nations that lost World War II. The Mexico City games saw the students rebel in the streets and some black athletes demonstrate. She is sorry for a recurrence of political and racial problems at the Munich games.

"It is still politics in the games," she said. "I am so sorry for it. I am sorry for the athletes who want only to compete. Every country will have the intention to show its political strengths and make political demonstrations. People did not learn from 1936. Not so much has changed."

The Sidelines' Other Side

Even for the athlete, there may be profit in seeing yourself as others see you.

Joe Crisco and Joe Tuna

January, 1971

This is a tale about two tourists named Joe who found fame, if not fortune, in Miami Beach.

These two working-stiff Joes had come all the way from Chicago to help close Tropical Park, to help open Hialeah, to cheer on Dallas in the Super Bowl, and on the last night of their four-day stay, to go to Tony's Fish Market for some pompano. They never made it to Tony's.

Their collision with fame began on the Sunday night after the Super Bowl when, on their way to Tony's, a Mercedes-Benz banged into their rented car. The Joe driving (known to his pal as "Charley Tuna" because he is such a fish on the golf course) climbed out to check the damage.

There wasn't much, except for the busted radiator in the Mercedes. As both parties exchanged licenses and waited for the cops, the other driver said he was Carroll Rosenbloom and he was owner of the Baltimore Colts.

"I do not care who you are," said Joe Tuna, "but if you are, then you cost us a lot of money. We took Dallas. Besides that, we paid 40 bucks apiece for 15-buck tickets."

"Gee," said Rosenbloom, "I'm sorry. You should have got in touch with me before the game."

"We did not know you before the game," recalled Joe Tuna.

The other Joe, Joe Crisco (he's called that because he is fat in the can), suggested they get a quick beer across the street while they waited. Rosenbloom had a better idea. He and his passenger, Gino Marchetti, were headed to this country club for the Colts' victory party, and the Joes were invited. Everyone thought that a fine idea. Rosenbloom then mentioned that these two Joes in open-collared flowered shirts might repair to their hotel and put on ties.

But the Joes said that to go back to the hotel, then way out to the party would take too much time because they were leaving for Chicago on the 4 A.M. plane.

"Well, then come over now," said Rosenbloom. And since his automobile was on the bum, he and Marchetti piled into the Joes' car.

"We thought we would drop in for a little swally," Joe Tuna said later.

But they stayed longer. They had steak dinner in an elegant dining room with candlelights at the table. They sat at the same table with several Colts, including Gino and Johnny Unitas, and they looked around a lot and always had a pitcher of beer in front of them.

They also had a Super Bowl program and Joe Crisco, who is not the retiring type, would call out, "Hey Bubba. Bubba, how 'bout an autograph?"

Joe Tuna said he called home to talk to his 18-year-old boy who is a Colts' fan and who would not believe this. "He was not home so I talked to my 90-year-old ma," said Joe Tuna.

" 'Ma,' I say, 'Guess where I am.'

" 'Jail,' she says.

" 'No, ma.' I say, 'I am at the Baltimore Colts' victory party."

"And she says, 'But Joe, I thought you bet on Dallas.' "

No sooner had he hung up than another unexpected guest popped in. It was Muhammad Ali. Joe Crisco wanted to clobber him. "But my pal here held me back," said Joe Crisco. "I do not have anything against Clay except I wanted to show him my left. That's my best punch."

"If Clay had started something I would of let Joe hit him," said Joe Tuna. "But I did not want Joe starting it."

After supper the others at the table left to mingle. The two Joes sat alone, the candlelight throwing shadows on their faces. They drank their beer and more and more looked into their steins and now and then glanced at their watches. Joe Tuna and Joe Crisco would soon have to excuse themselves from the victory party because they had a plane to catch.

Freddie Menna's Lost Art

February, 1969

Almost single-handedly, Freddie Menna is trying to revive the lost art of fight managing. It is not an easy thing to do, even for someone with the creativity, the endurance and the will of Freddie Menna.

Freddie and Rocky Graziano, both former middleweights, are partners in the Physical Arts gym in Freeport, Long Island. They are old friends and have boxed over 4,000 rounds together. Freddie, stocky, dark haired and a bit sad eyed, runs the place.

"We got quite a stable here, me and Rocky," said Freddie. "Twenty fighters, and four or five of 'em are college kids. That's unusual, y'know. They got pretty fair brains. What I mean is, they can talk without the words banging into each other.

"Managing ain't so easy as you think. I don't know, sometimes I just can't control fighters. And poof—they are gone. Some of 'em could have been the greatest fighters in the world, and the world covers a lot of places.

"There was one they brought to me. I looked at him 6-foot-

2,210. Irish. Beautiful build. Fantastic. They told me the Jets wanted him. He was All-Suffolk County in football and basketball and what not. Looks like he could be the greatest of all time.

"I don't know nothing about football but they said he was terrific. Could run the 100 in 9.1 in full uniform. Like I said, I don't know football but I imagine that is pretty good. Well, we put the kid in the corner to see what kind of chin he got, what kind of guts he got.

"You never know until they get the real thing. Some of 'em once they get hit turn yellow in a hurry. Like these karate guys who kick like mules and then get into a real battle on a dark street and they run like a thief.

"Well, there was no one for this guy to fight this day. So my trainer, Gene Moore—the best in the business—he says to me, 'You.' 'Me?' I can still handle myself O.K., but the guy looked like some giant. Well, I did. We get into a clinch. He picks me up like a toy. I finally get down, step one foot back and counter with a left to the chin.

" 'Oh, my God,' he says. And he falls to the floor. There went my one million dollars.

"Believe it or not, there's one thing you can't do with fighters. That's give 'em money. I had one guy, 6-feet-5, 240. Imagine! Oh, my goodness, here is my Great White Hope I said to myself. He was All-American, too. On my say-so the Royal Candle Company of New Jersey paid him $150 a week to train—that's the biggest candle company in America. So? He turns out to be a lush. His first fight he gets knocked out in the first round. It hurts me more than it hurts him, the lush.

"I found another champion on a schoolyard, playing basketball. He was a 19 year old, 6-3, 220. Gorgeously built He looked very terrific. But he was a Black Muslim and wouldn't fight white guys. Then I had a German heavyweight who thought he was Max Schmeling. He had two brains. Once he knocked out a Negro and then spit on him. It caused a riot. He'd say to his wife, 'I'm handsome. I'm nice, huh?' Then he had a fight and got knocked out, and I broke three smelling salts trying to wake him up.

"Another time I had this real clean-living fellow. Oh, was he something! The next Marciano. I'm all enthused. We trained for six months, and one day he comes to me and tells me he's going to be a priest. I begged and pleaded with him that he could not do this to me. I told him about the bees and the birds. But he says, 'The Lord is closer to me.'

"But there was another guy I had, you never seen nothing like it. I cannot even describe what this guy looked like. A walking mountain. And he said he's not scared of nobody. He would pound his chest like Tarzan.

"His first fight, I take him to Scranton. The bell rings and he takes two steps and falls. He wasn't even hit. He fainted."

John Amos: Least Wanted

January, 1973

John Amos surely holds the international record for having been cut from more football teams that any man who has ever had nose and nose-guard mashed in the mud. Yet he still maintains he was "very underrated, man."

Amos is 32 years old now. He has of course gone on to other things, being a grown man. He has become a television star (of *Good Times*) and movie actor (a recent picture is Walt Disney's *The World's Greatest Athlete,* in which he plays not the athlete—since he did not cast parts—but the coach).

His pursuit of pigskin glory is no longer a frustrating reality. It is a frustrating memory.

"Oh man, you won't believe it," Amos says, his eyes taking on a rather frenzied aspect. "But every time I was on the threshold of greatness, something unbelievable happened."

Amos began lugging his football dream around when he was a high school fullback on a losing team in East Orange, New Jersey. He sweet-talked his way into a full scholarship at Long Beach (California) City College. He had it figured that after he made Little All-American he would be sought after by every major college football power.

One day at practice the coach yelled at Amos. "Don't scream at me," Amos yelled back. The coach told him that he had a bad attitude and gave him the boot, thus launching the most spectacularly unsuccessful football career in history.

Amos learned that Colorado State University had the longest losing streak in college football. Amos figured that this was the place for him. "I got to be a star here. Right?" Not entirely.

Amos moved up to second team. He was also among those players complaining of too little meat at the training table. In the locker room a couple days before the game against the University of Pacific, Amos, experiencing creative urges in other areas, wrote a limerick on the blackboard: "*If U. of P. / We would beat / We would need / Much more meat.*" Back to third team, after the coach strolled in.

In the next game, the coach called for Amos along the sideline. This was it! Amos came crashing over, furiously trying to button his helmet. "The adrenalin was flowing," he recalls. "I could hear my friends in the stands screaming and yelling for me." The coach said, "Amos, give Pigears Hinton your shoulder pads, he just broke his."

The handwriting clearly on the wall, Amos decided to bestow his talents on the University of Denver. When the University of Denver heard the good news they dropped football.

All this was prologue to Amos's loftiest goal: pro ball. He

called the Denver Broncos, asked them for a tryout in the fall. Denver, desperate, agreed. That summer Amos worked construction, wearing lead vest and ankle weights to build himself up. After each grueling day, he'd work out at night, doing windsprints, lifting weights.

"Nobody on this planet was in better shape than me," he said. "Razor sharp."

But on the first day of practice Amos ran onto the field and pulled a hamstring muscle. "I had overtrained," he bitterly recalls. He tried to conceal his limp, but when he was clocked running the 40 in about two hours the coaches grew suspicious. Snip.

Next came the Canton (Ohio) Bulldogs in the United Football League. "This was where pro football began, the team Jim Thorpe played for, where the Pro Football Hall of Fame is," said Amos. "I went to the Hall of Fame every day, watching the films of the great players, touching the uniforms on display—I tried to turn myself into a star this way." Once again, though, he yanked his hamstring.

As Jitterbug Jones (who had also been cut from Canton) and Amos drove back West, they stopped in Joliet, Illinois, where the Joliet Explorers, the worst team in the United Football League, were holed up. "When I came into town the fever returned," said Amos.

When the Explorers met the Wheeling, West Virginia, team, Amos ran up against Pigears Hinton again. Amos got wind that Pigears had given a succinct scouting report on Amos. Pigears held his nose. Amos went on to gain 142 yards and score three touchdowns in that game. "Every time I scored a TD I bugalooed, I frugged, I jumped around in the end zone. I banged the ball to the ground. 'How you like that Pigears!' I screamed. 'Stuff that in your nose!'

"Now I'm about 24 or something. I still got the dream. I know I can go all the way, man. So I call Hank Stram. Why not?" Stram is coach of the Kansas City Chiefs. Amos gets the tryout. "As I ran onto the field just before the first exhibition game, against Denver, guess what? My hamstring goes again."

Kansas City cuts him. The Norfolk (Virginia) Neptunes cut him. Then he tears his Achilles' tendon with Wheeling, and Wheeling bids him adieu. When the tendon heals Amos rings up Stram, who has not been waiting breathlessly for the call. Yet Amos gets a second chance with the Chiefs.

"Well, I'm so obsessed with making the team that I'm tight," said Amos. "I can't remember the plays." Gone again.

He leaves the country, understandably. The Toronto Rifles, however, trade him to the Brooklyn Dodgers before he has a chance to get in a game. And the Dodgers drop him hastily, too.

"Now I'm about 25 or 26, I'm not sure at this point," he said. "I hear the Victoria (British Columbia) Steelers need help. They are the losingest team in Canada. I have trouble at customs. My hairline is receding by this time and I tell the official I'm a football player. He thinks I'm a bum."

Amos is the oldest guy on the team. Everyone else is making $50 a game. They offer Amos $25. He and his pride are next seen on the practice field of the Vancouver (British Columbia) Lions. The rule with U.S. imports is that they must be given a minimum four-day tryout. Amos is cut in two days.

It was the final hint. Amos reluctantly decided that football is for other people.

Vince Lombardi II

December, 1972—(Around Super Bowl time, the late Vince Lombardi is always news. First, he coached the winning team in the first two Super Bowls ever played. Second, the winning team now receives the Vince Lombardi Trophy.

And Lombardi lives in another way. Perhaps no other coach has had the impact on the philosophy of modern-day coaches—from Little League to the NFL—that Lombardi has had.)

"It's hard, really, to be me," said Vince Lombardi II. "Father is with me all the time—constantly. People miss him. People always remind you of that. But under no circumstances do I try to be his carbon copy. I'm a product of my generation, he was a product of his. My philosophy is different from his."

Possibly the most legendary bit of philosophy held by Vince Lombardi, the late Green Bay Packer and Washington Redskin coach, is that "Winning isn't everything—it's the only thing."

"A lot of people question that now," said Vince Lombardi II, in his law office in Minneapolis. "I guess I'm not willing to sacrifice all that he did for winning. Like I'm not willing to be from my family as much as he was. He had his way. I have mine."

Lombardi, now 30 years old, was recently elected to the Minnesota House of Representatives. His party affiiliation was Independent, but he said he will caucus with the Conservatives. He represents the Lino Lakes suburban area, where he lives with his wife and three boys, ages 6, 5, and 1½, and one daughter, 4.

"I guess parents always say that they will bring up their children different from their parents," said Lombardi. "So did I. For one thing, I was not going to be as physical with my kids as father was with me, not as strict. He was not one to spare the rod." Lombardi laughed. "Where did he hit me? Anywhere he could catch me.

"But I find myself saying some of the same things to my kids—'If I get hold of you you won't sit down for a week!'

"The thing he emphasized most was schoolwork. If I fell down in grades, he wouldn't let me out of the house until the next marking period. I had nothing to do except study. But I remember one time I was a sophomore in high school, when we still lived in New Jersey. I got thrown out of school for a day, for a very minor matter. I was told to bring my father and mother to see the principal the next day.

"I was really in trepidation, waiting for my father to come home. When I told him what happened, he didn't say 'boo.' I was steeling myself for the worst. But he knew that I felt bad enough, so he didn't have to say anything. He had a great sense of timing. Though I wish he had been a little more nonphysical like that a little more often."

When Lombardi was 16, his father got the head coaching job at Green Bay, and so the family of four (including a younger sister) moved to Wisconsin. It was here that young Vince began to feel the pressures of being the son of a legend-to-be.

"I played football and the report around the high school, a Catholic school named Premontre, was that I was supposed to be the greatest thing since sliced bread," Lombardi recalled. "They figured, if he's the coach's son, he's got to be great. They had me up to 6 feet 2, when at my very best I was 5 feet 10, 195."

Lombardi became a starting fullback on the team, yet he felt his father never really cared very much.

"I'd come home and I'd say, 'Dad, I scored a touchdown today.' He'd say, 'Oh yeah?' I thought he wasn't interested in me as an athlete only as a student. But later I'd hear that he was pleased when I did well on the football field.

"In retrospect, I guess it was good that he never pressured me to be an athlete. He probably sensed that there was enough pressure on me—by myself and by others—and he didn't want to add. Everyone expected big things of me, including me, because I was Vince Lombardi's son. I used to feel very, very tense before games."

Lombardi received a football scholarship to St. Thomas College in St. Paul, Minnesota. He eventually became a starting fullback and captain of the football team. One of the few times he remembers his father interceding in his college career was at the beginning of his sophomore year.

"I took a room off campus," said Lombardi. "Father called the dean of men and told him to send me home. He didn't want me living off campus. Well, I got a room in a dormitory."

Lombardi recalls something else about college days. "I may have been the only kid in school who hated to go home for summer vacation." Lombardi laughed again. "Father always found the hardest jobs for me to do at home—construction, loading boxes into semitrailers in a pickle factory. He made it a point never to find me an easy job.

"He learned about the value of hard work from his father. My grandfather was strict, too, in the ways of the old country. I remember father saying that he always had to do a lot of busy work around the house. They lived in Brooklyn but they had a barn, and father remembered having to tear up the barn floor and then his father made him put the planks down again. And it had to be a good job! Or my grandfather would be mad and get physical."

"So father learned early the philosophies that would carry him through his life: appealing to an individual's pride, integrity, singleness of purpose, commitment to excellence—winning.

"Some of those things I have accepted and live by, too. But there are pluses and minuses. I had great respect for my father. I was in awe of him. And because of this we weren't what you'd call buddies, never really the closest. He was dedicated to his work—and he was a great success at it. But he wasn't home that much. He was very busy. We'd talk on occasion, but you mostly had to fend for yourself.

"But life was exciting, to be in the center of it. And for a kid, to go to training camp with a pro football team—wow!

"I saw that his philosophies at home were the same with his football team. He drove them like he tried to drive me. But he was also aware that everyone's an individual. He had to take everything into proper context. He has been a great influence on a lot of coaches—not just in the pros—but on the lower levels, down to pre-high school football coaches. And from what I've seen and heard, I'm not convinced that younger kids are prepared for the strain that some well-meaning coaches place on them. Maybe you can't overemphasize the striving for excellence, but I think you can overemphasize the striving for victory.

"What made father so unusual was that he was so articulate and so successful. And you know, it wasn't until his last year or so of life that he realized that he had more to offer people than just football. He realized that people wanted to hear the things he had to say about malcontents and misfits receiving too much emphasis when the achievers and doers should get it. He was surprised at the impact.

"One thing I take a tremendous amount of satisfaction in is that father didn't realize his dream of becoming a head pro coach until he was 46 years old. I think of this when I'm feeling impatient about not having accomplished all I've wanted. And I'm only 30. So father's greatest example for me, possibly, is that you've got to serve your apprenticeship —put in your time, make your mistakes."

Son of Ty Cobb

Washington, July, 1969

James Cobb sat at lunch and he had a book of baseball players' records and he was saying that his hobby was statistics.

"Here," he said, his fingers crooked into two parts of the book, "take a look at the totals, just take a look."

This was after Babe Ruth had been selected the Greatest Player of All-Time by the baseball writers, and Ty Cobb, James Cobb's father, was presumably second to Ruth. The two pages James Cobb had under scrutiny were the lifetime records of Babe Ruth and Ty Cobb.

"Look at the number of hits," he said. It read: Cobb 4,191, Ruth 2,873. "And the batting averages." Cobb .367, Ruth .342. "And runs scored." Cobb 2,244, Ruth 2,174. Cobb also had more doubles, 724 to 506, and more triples, 297 to 136. But Ruth, of course, was several thousand light years ahead of Cobb in home runs, 714 to 118 and had more runs-batted-in, 2,209 to 1,954.

"I was only seven years old," said James Cobb, "when dad retired in 1928 and I don't remember him playing. But his record is the best, and people tell me the things he did were fantastic, like going from first to third on an infield out."

James Cobb's involvement with baseball is limited to

working with youngsters in Santa Maria, California, his home town, and with representing his father—who died eight years ago—at awards ceremonies. He works as an expediter at Lockheed.

"I think there's a jinx with sons of famous athletes," he said. "None of them ever topped their fathers. Look at Dick Sisler and Big Ed Walsh's son. They never did make it real big. And I understand Stan Musial's son was a very good baseball player. But he gave it up."

Ty Cobb never pressed his three sons (Hershel and Ty, Jr., died in early manhood) to be athletes. But James Cobb remembers the pride his father took in James's achievements. James is 5 foot 7, some five inches shorter than his father, and he feels that was one reason he amounted to little as an athlete.

"But I remember once playing junior high school touch football and the coach was about to substitute for me," he said. "But just then he saw dad arrive at the field and he decided to leave me in. Well, I blocked a punt and recovered it. I looked over at dad and he put up a fist, as if to say, 'Thataway to go, son.' I was on top of the world. The next day a local newspaper headline read: 'Son Blocks Punt as Father Watches'."

James would also pitch to his father in their back yard. "I got so," said James Cobb, "where dad had to put a handkerchief in his glove to keep the swelling down."

Though Ty Cobb, a strict disciplinarian, rarely complimented his boys on their athletic feats, James recalled an incident when he was "playing possum," pretending to be asleep on the living room couch and he overheard his dad say to a friend, "Little Jimmy's got a pretty good ol' curve ball."

James said that he feels it unfair when people say his father had no friends and was a morose man. "He was nice to people and he had a good sense of humor," said James. "I remember Gabby Street coming to the house often and he and dad reminiscing—sometimes I'd be awakened at three in the morning by their laughter."

Ty Cobb rarely talked to his sons about his days as a player, except for one thing. James said his father was proudest of being the first man selected for the Hall of Fame. "He used to show me the clippings," said James, "where he got 211 out of a possible 214 votes."

One point Cobb did emphasize to his children (he had two daughters, also) was good grades. "He read a lot, like the news magazines and books," said James, "and he always wanted us to do well in school. He would deprive us of things if our grades didn't meet his approval. He always wanted us to work as hard as we could at anything we did. Just as he did.

"I remember in 1942 he was to play three golf matches against Babe Ruth as part of a war bond drive. About three months before the first match dad began practicing. Every day, putting, driving, chipping. Hour after hour.

"And during the matches he would do everything he could to win and to upset the Babe—he would come late, cough when the Babe was lining up a putt, walk around him this way, then that. Dad beat Babe two out of three."

Bruce Dern: The Mad Jogger

New Orleans, December, 1968

His long blondish hair flapped a bit madly in the wind and his eyes, while not exactly wild, did possess a glint of uncommon joy. So naturally the cops stopped him as he trotted past the local mental institution.

"Hello," greeted one of the New Orleans officers. "Where are you off to on this lovely morning?"

"To work," he replied, running in place. "I'm an actor."

"How nice. Where is work?"

"La Place. We're shooting there today."

"Hmmmm. That's 32 miles away. How will you get there?"

"Run."

"Of course."

While one of the policemen continued talking with the man, the other dropped in briefly at the institution. To his satisfaction, no patient had run away that day. So the cops booked Bruce Dern on general principles. The case was dismissed in court.

Dern, 32, is one of the leads in a football movie, *Pro,* starring Charlton Heston. The New Orleans Saints have cooperated with the studio, and the set location was there. Dern is also a long distance runner, competitively and pleasurably.

He is the American champion in the 40-mile and 42-mile runs but is quite humble about his accomplishments. When asked his times, he lowers a lid and says, "Times are really unimportant because there are not many other nuts who run that distance."

As a New Trier High School track star, primarily in the half mile, he made the Illinois High School Hall of Fame. At the University of Pennsylvania he never lost a race. He still does not lose many races, but his track record against dogs and cops is not so sterling.

When he suits up for a biff across hill and dale, he arms himself with stones. "To discourage dogs from getting too friendly," he said. "Sometimes they will follow me, yipping and snapping for miles. But they usually turn back before they get too far from home."

People of all sorts give him the fish-eye and worse, when they observe him loping by. "Surfers in California are the meanest," he said. "I will be running on a highway, and they will often swerve their cars at me. They find all the puddles, too. Some folks just don't like others to do something they don't do. It scares them."

In Alabama, people asked whom he was running from. In Texas, they stared in disbelief, and some hopped in cars to follow out of morbid curiosity.

In New Orleans, Dern found occasion to wing around the block 100 or so times every night. Across from his hotel was a fire station, and a fireman, sitting in front, noted this activity with interest. Finally, he called, "Hey, buddy, where's the fire?"

Dern is also a very dependable fellow to have working for you. He is always on hand, or on foot, as it happens. Producer Walter Seltzer called his home once and asked if Dern could run over for a chat. Fourteen miles and a couple hours later he toddled through the door, puffing only slightly.

He has been arrested 17 times and fined over $100 for kicking up his legs in public.

Not long ago a Beverly Hills policeman said Dern was loitering. "Loitering is when you are standing around," protested Dern. "I am moving."

At the time Dern was training for the Olympic marathon team (he did not make it because, among other things, work conflicted with workouts). This night he wore his USA track suit. The cop wanted to know what the lettering stood for. Dern inquired what the BHPD on the officer's hat stood for. Booked again.

Al Toefield: Big Wheel

June, 1972

Members of the U.S. Olympic cycling team will readily cough up the information that where there's smoke there's Alfred Toefield. Alfred Toefield is a New York City police sergeant who was accused by some cyclists of puffing cigar smoke in their faces during the road-racing qualifying run at Lake Luzerne, New York.

Toefield is also chairman of the Olympic cycling committee. He was following on motorcycle the 67 bike riders over the 120-mile course. He followed them slowly (puffingly) up a mountainside; he followed them at a 60-miles-an-hour plummet down and round hairpin curves; he was following to determine which of the helmeted riders had Olympian qualities of aggressiveness, cool-headedness, courage and pedal power.

"Some of 'em are on a big ecology kick, so they say I'm polluting the air," said Toefield. "They make a thing of my cigar smoking. But they're kidding.

"They know I need an outlet for my nervousness. They know I can't take it out on the pedals like them. So I chew the hell out of my cigar."

Toefield, one hot New York morning, explained this while wiping his square-jawed face with a pink paper towel. He sat in his small office, the decor of which is highlighted by a flyswatter on his cluttered desk and packets of Alka-Seltzer and a heartburn remedy clipped to cardboard on the wall.

When Sgt. Alfred Toefield is not chairing the cycling committee, he is working with youth gangs, which is why on this warm day he sat with V-necked T-shirt and sneakers. But lately he has spent much time and energy trying to pare down the qualifiers for the 10 track and 8 road cyclists he will trundle off to Munich.

"So I've been like Speedy Gonzales," he said. "I clean up my blotter and hustle off, say, to San Jose to check on the track qualifiers. We're going to have one of our best teams in years, and we've got a lot of top-notch riders to pick from. It's not like it used to be, where we were second-class athletes. Cyclists here are starting to get dignity."

One reason for the new "dignity" is the great resurgence of popularity that cycling has achieved in this country. Another factor for the rise in dignity among cyclists in Sgt. Alfred Toefield.

Since the days when bicycles were built for two and guys wanted to marry a girl just like the girl that married dear old dad, cyclists had come under public opprobrium. Motorists and cops alike believed that bicycles and baby buggies should be kept on sidewalks. Cops ticketed cyclists; motorists took devilish delight in running them off the road.

Now, with a growing concern for ecology, bicycles are considered to be better than cars as far as congestion, pollution, taxes, accidents, and exercise are concerned.

Toefield has also contributed greatly to the image and growth of cycle racing here. Once a cyclist himself, he has for 25 years hustled money from amateur groups and bicycle manufacturers to aid cycle clubs and the Olympic team. He says one of his proudest achievements was getting New York officials to open Central Park for the 1960 Olympic cycling qualifying run. "It was the first time in history that Central Park was closed to vehicular traffic," he said.

When Toefield's team is assembled he will insist (as he did in '68 and in the last two Pan-Am Games) that his team adhere to strict codes: curfew is usually at 10 P.M.; dress is standard (he makes the cyclists send home all "civilian" clothes). He denies that he runs a "mini" police state.

"What I do is to enhance our image abroad," he says. "I don't want people from other countries thinking that the American is obnoxious."

Toefield says that his committee is the only one to send an Olympic member home from the Games. That happened in Mexico City four years ago. Dave Mulky, according to Toefield, broke training rules. "He disputed the idea that we knew more about what was good for him than he did," said Toefield.

One thing Toefield is certain is good for everyone is cycling. "The more we do it," he said, "the healthier we'll be as a nation.

"Like the story I heard the other day, supposed to be true. A big gruff executive was told by his doctor that he should ride to work on a bike. The first day he does it, this business tycoon is feeling so good that he comes bounding into the office for the first time in history, says, 'Good morning, everybody!' Four secretaries fainted."

Charles Miron: Highest Scorer in the History of Half-Court Basketball

May, 1972

Charles Miron may be the highest scorer in the history of half-court basketball.

Charles said he passed the 170,000-point mark not long ago. (By comparison, Wilt Chamberlain is the all-time NBA leader with less than 30,000 points). Charles said that not even Bob Cousy or Dick McGuire—two other half-court aces he has played with—could have scored as many, since they were corrupted by the full-court game.

It is even more points than Lou Goldstein ever scored. Goldstein was once a marvelous half-court player until he virtually retired a few seasons back to lead the "Simon Says" games at Grossinger's resort in the Catskills.

Charles, who is 6 foot 2, 200 pounds and wears fuzzy, graying muttonchops on a dapper if baldish head, said he has played half-court in "all the basketball capitals of the world," from Indianapolis to Stockholm, from Beverly Hills to Brooklyn. He has played several games a day for at least 200 days a year for 30 years. He has a superb left-handed set shot, though he does not go to his right all that well.

Half-court basketball is the national game of New York City, where Charles was born, reared, and still lives and plays. The game, as played in New York, has three on a side, seven baskets wins, scorers out. (That is, if your team makes a basket, you get the ball out again). Other areas have variations on that theme.

"The Cousys and McGuires were great half-court players," said Charles. "In fact, Bob played the pivot. But there were guys as great or even greater who never made it in college or the pros. The reason is that half-court is a whole different ball game. It's an individual's game. First guy gets the ball shoots.

"There were guys who could do all the shticks like Cousy, but they couldn't do it with four other guys. They couldn't work patterns. A guy like Dave Mantz could do anything Pete Maravich could do. His problem was that he couldn't make a simple layup. He'd drive in and then loop it over his head. He went to college, and he was throwing full-court, beind-the-back blind passes. One day the coach just bid him farewell. But Dave is still unstoppable in the California playgrounds.

"Another of the great half-courters was a guy named Rabbit Walthour. He was up with the Milwaukee Hawks. He liked to shoot a running hook without looking from the top of the key. He played four games and was gone. Wound up in Sing Sing. Narcotics. He had to adjust there and became a very good full-court player, I hear.

"A lot of guys had great reputations as half-courters, but some were made on playgrounds where there was a dead spot in the backboard. These kings went to another court and usually were wiped out. The Mecca of the playgrounds in New York was Rockaway Beach, where the McGuire brothers played. On a Sunday it was so crowded that if you lost you had fifth next—the day was practically shot waiting around.

"Games were tough at Rockaway. In other places, a defensive ace would say, 'I held my man to two shots.' At Rockaway, someone like Tricky Dick McGuire would say, 'I held my man to two *passes*.'

"I still play because I love it. You never get your name in the paper, and I've never seen a great half-courter who played for pretty chicks, either, like a lot do in college. But you play for within yourself.

"And any guy who tells you he doesn't know how much he's scored in a game is dishonest. He knows. Me, I've scored over 170,000 points, roughly. And that's without shooting free throws, because you don't shoot them in half-court. But I'm a terrific free-throw shooter, too. I can shoot 90 per cent all day. But I know it's a developed skill that's of no real value."

Highpockets in the Bleachers

Chicago, July, 1970

The renowned Bleacher Bums, who have actually incorporated, have brought a new look to the cozy one-buck seats in the Wrigley Field outfield. Besides their bright yellow construction helmets, they have inadvertently cleaned up the joint.

"These guys have gotten so much publicity," said Highpockets, "that the bleachers aren't safe for the common man any more. The TV cameras are always poking around out there in the afternoon now. And a lot of guys who were supposed to be at funerals had to dive under the seats.

"And these Bleacher Bums, with all their beer drinking, got a lot of bulls to come circulating. You can't make a bet like you used to. The old days are gone."

Highpockets, like Moulin Rouge and the Junk Man and others of their adventurous bent, has been coming to Cub games in the bleachers for years, in those long losing years, to enjoy the society of men who know baseball as a science.

"Now," he said, "you come to the park early to see batting practice, and maybe you're in bad shape from the night before, and all you hear are the kids beating drums and the Bums' practice cheers. There's no one to talk baseball and the betting line with anymore.

"Before, you'd come out early to get a jump on things. I mean, what if you saw the probable starting pitcher running in the outfield. You knew he wouldn't be pitching. You'd make a beeline for a phone.

"And what a grand bunch of fellows we were. Actually, there were two cliques. There were the guys who sat under the scoreboard in the shade. They were called 'ghosts.' The rest of us sat in the sun. Gamblers usually like sun like everyone else, makes 'em look like millionaire playboys. But we all knew baseball like scientists. Odds were figured from inning to inning, depending on the score, on who was pitching—on his percentage of complete games—on the strength of the bullpen, and who had relieved recently. These guys didn't need record books.

"In the old days, just a few years ago, you'd hold up fingers to a friend, like three fingers, and he'd raise his eyebrows. And you knew you were on, 3-1, on a hundred bucks. It was like the commodities exchange.

"And there'd be so many bets going that to keep track a guy'd have a lot more on his scorecard than just runs, hits, errors. Money wouldn't be passed around in the open. But it looked strange that guys who saw each other every day would shake hands eight times a game.

"Or after a game someone would walk into the men's room and wonder why three guys were together in a stall.

"There was honor among thieves, so to speak. You might stiff your neighborhood bookie for a grand. But you'd never stiff a guy in the bleachers for even a fin. Or else you could never show your face there again. And I'll never forget Old Sambo. He's dead now. But he was an old-timer who talked about seeing games when the Cubs played at the old West Side park. Once, he left the park in the eighth inning. He was sure he'd won an 'ice-box' game. I mean, a cinch. He was already walking down Sheridan Road when he passed a bar. He heard cheering from the television set. And somehow the game got tied up. He came all the way back, in time to see Ernie Banks hit a homer in the 11th inning. He came up with all the dough, right then.

"When some of the fellows see each other now and we

talk about the old days and about Old Sambo, we say that cancer, or whatever he had, didn't kill him as much as Banks's home run that day."

Ode to Marianne Moore

February, 1972

Marianne Moore viewed sport as it ought to be, and soaringly more. "It is a legitimate triumph as a feat of skill, like writing," she once said.

She valued "self-mastery" and the joy of deep involvement: "I'm foolish about Willie Mays. He is just full of intellectual energy. He kind of lets everything go for the end in view. Quite scientific, and he certainly gets around the bases!"

Marianne Moore, a slight (5 foot 3½), gray-haired woman who favored tricorn hats, died on February 5 at age 84. She was one of America's most celebrated poets. "Her work," T. S. Eliot has said, "is a part of the small body of durable poetry written in our time." She possessed a captivating genius to see and delight in the interweaving of seeming disparities.

In her poem, "Baseball and Writing," she said: "Writing is exciting / and baseball is like writing / you can never tell with either / how it will go / or what you will do."

"Yes," she said in an interview a few years ago, "sport has its counterpart in life, and I can hardly credit a person who thinks sport is mindless. An 'intellectual' who is above sports really isn't an intellectual."

She saw that "sound technique is indispensable to the musician, painter, engineer, mechanic, athlete, fencer, boxer." She could be "carried away" by grace of performance. About the great race horse Tom Fool, she wrote:

"Tom Fool is 'a handy horse,' with a chiseled foot. You've the beat / of a dancer to a measure or harmonious rush / of a porpoise at the prow where the racers all win easily—/ like centaurs' legs in tune, as when kettle-drums compete; / nose rigid and suede nostrils spread, a light left hand on the / rein, till/well—this is rhapsody."

"Fortitude," "finesse," "equipoise," "expertness," "the miracle of dexterity," were highly admired by Marianne Moore. She became a solid Dodger fan when watching the "vim" with which Roy Campanella went about his catching chores: "I remember his walking back to the mound to give some earnest advice to the pitcher, Karl Spooner. Then Roy hastened back to the plate. His brisk, confident roll was very prepossessing and I thought, 'I guess I'll have to keep an eye on him.' "

She knew several top athletes personally. The first was Jim Thorpe. In a quirk of fate, Marianne Moore taught typing and shorthand at the Carlisle (Pennsylvania) Indian School. Thorpe was her student in 1912 and 1913.

"James was the most pleasant athlete to watch," she said. "He was so limber and could perform wonderful feats with the grace of a leopard, and then take no credit for his achievements. A very unaffected person. And, you know, he wrote an old-fashioned Spencerian hand, very deliberate and elegant."

She once met Muhammed Ali in a restaurant, and the boxer took her outside and demonstrated his "Ali Shuffle." "Magnificent," she recalled. She developed a friendship with Floyd Patterson, respected his triumph over a troubled youth. Wrote Marianne Moore about Patterson's autobiography, *Victory Over Myself*: "The victory involved 'application and concentration'—age-old formula for results in any kind of work, profession, art, recreation—'powerful feeling and the talent to use it!' "

Perhaps she understood so well the struggles and joys of mind and body in orchestration because she herself had participated in sports.

On learning to ride a bicycle as a teen-ager: "Riding itself was hard, but I delighted in sweeping down smooth roads and looking at trees in blossom. That was worthwhile." She once played tennis almost every day, and often her face "would become scarlet because I was trying so hard. . . . But I had to—after all, I would perish if I couldn't try hard.

"But in sport you must learn to accept grieving situations, like losing by a slight accident. That was nearly unbearable for me. But you can't cry on someone's shoulder. You can't ask people to give credit for what you don't do. Yet I like something I once read in the *Boston Transcript* about a scull race that Harvard had lost. The paper said, 'Win or lose, their speed is marvelous.' Harvard still was a winner in a sense."

In her 80s, in her small Greenwich Village apartment, Marianne Moore would still exercise by swinging from a bar in the doorway of her bedroom. She also had a photograph of Honus Wagner which she valued: "Whenever I'm despondent I turn to this picture. It puts me in good humor. Honus has a look here of impeccable optimism. Maybe that's too general, but he has no chip on his shoulder, not malicious in any way."

She was both buoyant and dogged, and found these traits inseparable from the pursuit of joy in sport and life. This was well-expressed in her pithy poem, "I May, I Might, I Must":

"If you will tell me why the fen / appears impassable, I then / will tell you why I think that I / can get across it if I try."

(All poetry excerpts from *The Complete Poems of Marianne Moore*, 1967, Macmillan Company and Viking Press.)

Jimmy Cannon: One Last Line

January, 1973

This is being written in hopes of keeping quick an anecdote concerning Jimmy Cannon, the doughty and splendid sportswriter who died recently at age 64.

I was standing with Jimmy on a simmeringly sunny day in Miami Beach, waiting for the press bus to take us from the hotel to the stadium, where we were covering the Super Bowl game.

The warm morning was already taking its toll on Jimmy's reddish, roundish face, speckled now with spots of sweat. The sun gleamed off his sunglasses, his baldish head, his brown loafers.

Coming up Collins Avenue, I noticed about 30 people, adults and children, on bicycles pedaling in our direction. They looked like several families going to a picnic. There were little pennants on the handlebars and lunch bags in the bike baskets.

I turned to Jimmy and said, "See that?"

He squinted and said in his side-of-the-mouth New York style, "Jee-sus Christ, look what inflation has done to the Hell's Angels."

An anecdote does not make the man (nor does a good line make a good novel, as Gertrude Stein once told Ernest Hemingway). But it can give a clue to the cut of a man's mind.

Jimmy's mind and heart were open to public view almost daily for several decades. His sports column appeared in

Hearst newspapers across the country. His pointed, passionate approach, his overflowing loves and hates, influenced a generation of sportswriters. He loved the dignity of a Joe DiMaggio, and despised frauds. Once, for example, a fighter who had taken a dive and whom Cannon blistered in print, tried to shake hands with Cannon in a restaurant. "I don't shake hands with creeps," said Cannon.

I only knew Jimmy in his later years, after his New York outlet, the *Journal-American*, had folded in 1967. People said Jimmy began to fold when that happened, since he was a product of Greenwich Village and part of an age of the New York night life of Toots Shor's, the Stork Club, Lindy's—of an age passed.

Though the death of the *Journal-American* may have drained some life out of him, I did not notice it. He was a man who lived for his work. He tried to enter men's souls by investigating their motivations. And he was a craftsman. He was proud of his profession and disdained the hacks. One time in the press box at Yankee Stadium, a guy rushed in and exclaimed that somebody had burned down the house of another New York sportswriter, a noted mediocrity.

"The arsonist must have been an English professor," said Cannon.

Hemingway was at once an admirer and gentle critic of Cannon's writing. Cannon once wrote that "Nothing pleased me more than when Ernest Hemingway picked my book, *Nobody Asked Me*, as one of the three best of the year."

Another time, Hemingway said that Jimmy's enthusiasm could trip him up periodically, that "Jimmy sometimes sets out to write a piece to end writing, and he's going to leave writing dead on the floor."

But when Cannon was good, he was grand. On Joe Louis: "He is a credit to his race—the human race."

His column of one-liner insights, *Nobody Asked Me, But*, was his trademark:

"The plainest of women look exciting in a polka-dotted dress."

"In my neighborhood, an old man wouldn't shake hands with an undertaker."

"I've never caught a circus clown I thought was funny."

"If Howard Cosell were a sport, he'd be the roller derby."

When I knew Jimmy, he seemed alone a lot. He was a lifelong bachelor, and there is always a sadness about such men, as if they are missing a dimension. Jimmy would tell you about a column he just wrote, and make you feel it was very important, until you walked away. Then you realized that it was his telling you about it that was so important. Or maybe it was your listening to his telling that was so important.

In some ways, he reminded me of the panhandler he once described who worked Park Avenue wearing a boutonniere.

Much of what he wrote dies with him, if it is not already long buried. For it is true that yesterday's newspapers are used to wrap fish.

But Jimmy's memory lives, at least with me. He and those Hell's Angels on bicycles.

Marcel Marceau: Sports and Art

New York, May, 1973

Marcel Marceau, the sublime and poignant mime, sees the Olympic events like this:

The javelin thrower thrusts back and gets his spear stuck in the mud.

The weight lifter, oppressed by his upraised burden, slowly sinks into a split.

The poised and crouched 100-meter-dash man's first step crunches his finger.

The shot-putter's ball falls on his foot.

The hip-wobbling walker runs out of steam, like a wind-up toy, and crumbles.

Originally, the organizers of the Munich Olympics had wanted Marceau to make a film pantomiming the various athletic events. The organizers would surely have agreed with a recent review of Marceau's wordless but stirring one-man show. "Marceau imitates life with an honesty that gives life a new dimension," wrote Clive Barnes in the *New York Times*.

But the film was never made. Olympic committee members believed that Marceau's satiric portrayals would pluck too sensitive a chord in light of the Olympic Village murders.

On stage, Marceau is white faced and primarily a comedian, but one who demonstrates marvelous athletic skills such as impossibly tilting his body as he leans on an invisible café counter. Like most comedians, however, he is serious and captures along with the foibles, the grace, the tragedy and the delight in life. The decision not to film Marceau's unique views of athletes and athletics was uninspired. It is an artistic deprivation not to share his insights into the world of muscle.

In Marceau's Plaza Hotel suite one morning, the silent mime spoke eloquently of sports and art.

He found the Olympic events dramatic, as well as surrealistically funny.

"The athlete," said the French mime, "must spend four years to prepare. But he must not overtrain. He must leave a mo-*ment* to surpass himself, to go beyond his own limits.

"He must be relieved from fear. Anxiety can kill possibility. There must be no thought of defeat. The skills, the beauty of line, the concentration can move me, even to tears.

"I remember seeing one Olympic gymnast who fractured his foot. But he continued to give his team points. He had to jump from the bar to execute his finale. He landed and received himself very well, straight and proud. Then he collapsed. It was heroic."

Marceau's favorite sports to observe are figure skating, gymnastics, and diving. "These I love," he said. "It is not just to win but how you win, the form, that counts. It is complete art."

He admires the Brazilian soccer players. "They are like jugglers," he said. "The ball never is on the floor." And of Pele, their star: "He is always noble. He is very orthodox, pure and never compromises. He would never do anything unfair just to be victorious."

He did not respect the way Bobby Fischer "ruthlessly destroyed his opponent. Fischer is a chess artist. But what he did was not beautiful."

The Harlem Globetrotters, though, have his admiration: "It is an act, of course, the way they fool very much the reflexes of their opponent. But the timing and the control is the greatest virtuosity."

"Weight-lifting," he says, "is monstrous. I admire the men but it is terrible to look at."

American football: "It is not noble. It is too efficient and too brutal."

Boxing can be magnificent, in his view. Sugar Ray Robinson, he said, was a grand stylist, and one who would never hit a *coup bas*—below the belt. And Joe Louis, though plodding, had the air of "a sovereign."

Muhammad Ali, at his best, is the epitome of athletic artistry for Marceau.

"He is cool," said Marceau, who requested a 4 A.M. hotel wake-up call in Hamburg, Germany, to watch the Ali-Joe Frazier title bout on television. "He has an elegance of line, a supreme confidence, and a profound concentration.

"He seemed to have complete control of himself in that fight. He was graceful and strong. Never gave a feeling of effort. The greatest artists keep a cool. There is little muscular sweat. They sweat because the concentration is so big or the arena is hot. It is the same with the great violinist. Or the tightrope walker. They sweat only when they are tense, and then they stumble.

"The great artist and champion goes beyond his own possibilities, beyond exhaustion. He reaches the *état de grâce*. He feels no pain. When Frazier hit Ali and made his legs rubber, Ali kept his dignity. He thought, 'Incredible—this cannot be happening to me.' He was like a grog-*gy*-sculpture, too proud to stay down.

"It is the mind behind that makes the great man. Ali proved in that fight that he was not afraid to die. He was fearless. He is also an enigma. Sometimes he is not so magnificent. But nobody can be great all the time. You would destroy yourself in the effort. But the real man, we don't know. Maybe Ali's power in boxing is that you cannot go behind his mind.

"Even in defeat, he is undefeated. He is, yes, a monument. Interesting."

End of the Grass Age

Forest Hills, New York, January, 1975

"It's like Guadalcanal," he said, and indeed it seemed a battle had been fought here.

In the wintry twilight, Owen Sheridan, the short, ruddy, head groundsman in knit cap, stood in the empty West Side Tennis Club stadium. A mauve sky with blackening clouds stretched across the concrete stadium's top. Leafless tree branches moved lightly in the wind, raking the concrete wall with an eerie whisper. A cat moaned in the catacombs.

On the field below, bulldozers hunched like abandoned tanks, their tough work appearing complete: the lovely, lush green of this once sacrosanct center court had been transformed into a wet and rutted mud field.

For the first time in more than half a century, the next United States tennis championships, in September, would be held not on grass but on a gray, clay composition court.

And the battle that raged for the past several years between traditonalists and "modernists" was ended now, in the mud below.

Owen Sheridan, 63 years old, has been tending these courts for 42 years, ever since he arrived from Ireland at 18 and took the first job he could get. He has spent his life tamping down divots, snapping up brown blades, manicuring and watering and fussing over virtually each inch of grass, the sod that since 1923 Tilden and Perry and Gonzales and Laver and Ashe and Newcombe, among men, and Wills and Jacobs and Gibson and King and Court and Evert, among women, have trod.

White-haired, undemonstrative Owen Sheridan, his face red and crinkly from the sun, would sit 30 feet away from center court, ready to make an immediate house call of sorts whenever an unsightly blemish popped up.

Sheridan has had a most intimate relationship with the grass. He says he would even talk to it. He had no horticultural or botanical background before taking the job. "But when you've been around grass for some time," he said, "the sod practically speaks to you. So you listen, and you give it what it asks for."

No more. He watched in the chill and barren January as the shovels went about their unsentimental chores.

"It's like watching 42 years of your life being dug up and

hauled off on a trook," said Owen Sheridan, who still has a little brogue. "I cry inside, to be truthful with ya."

For years he carried on the battle against crab grass and "fairy ring" (a mysterious grass ailment that often kills the greenery), and, since Forest Hills is in the New York City borough of Queens, he battled the air pollution that leaves a murderous residue of smoke and oil on the daintily pampered grass.

He also rooted against those players with the unsavory propensity to drag their feet, thus rutting up Sheridan's lawns.

"I tried my best," he said, "but then I'd read in the papers the next day about one player or another had lost and blamed my grass. He said the court stinks. I didn't care too much for that."

Complaints abounded that despite Sheridan's meticulous care, grass is just too unpredictable, too natural for play today, and bad bounces and slippery footing cannot be tolerated. The strong Association of Tennis Professionals, led by president Arthur Ashe, finally overcame grass enthusiasts who believed that the warm and charming atmosphere of grass games ought to be maintained in light of the growing cold artificiality of other spectator sports.

"But no," said Sheridan, "today tennis is a business. Those days of its being a sport are over. Every game means a lot of money. It was once like a nice social event. And, you know, opponents used to drop the next point when a bad call was made in their favor. You used to see quite a lot of that. You seldom see it anymore.

"Everybody's fighting to get on top."

The clay composition needs attention, like being daily brushed and rolled, and watered when it gets dusty, but the artistic and scientific challenge of having a unique problem daily with grass is over for Sheridan.

"This is progress, I suppose, and you've got to live with it," he said. "It's like having a wife who dies. You may not have got along too good with her, but you miss her. It's sad."

Owen Sheridan, the transplanted Irishman, happens to pronounce the word "sad" like "sod."

Dick Woit: The Healing Hun

January, 1975

You have to hate Dick Woit before you can love him.

In fact, you have to hate Dick Woit while you love him.

Dick Woit, physical director at the Lawson YMCA in Chicago, is a half-breed. Half Oral Roberts, half Attila the Hun.

A fellow named Stevie would eagerly agree. Two years ago, at age 19, Stevie was brought by his father to the place where Woit holds his incredible exercise classes. The room, just off the gym, is small, barracks green, and undeniably odoriferous.

Stevie clumped in with two canes and leg braces. He had suffered spinal deterioration. Physical therapists and acupuncturists had given up on him. He was giving up on himself. Woit was the last resort.

Woit looked Stevie over. Suddenly, Woit kicked away the canes; Stevie staggered and flailed. "Fall down and you ain't got the guts for my classes," hollered Woit. Stevie grabbed the wall. Didn't fall.

Stevie became a regular, happily taking the verbal abuse that is showered upon all of "Woit's Warriors"—the names printed on the T-shirts that they wear proudly, like badges of courage.

Familial and ethnic pejoratives are the sweetest phrases Woit intones to his chorus of grunters. Ignominious physical castigations are his staples.

But he is as dedicated a physical therapist and psychologist as he is a blue linguist. He took great pains, for example, with Stevie. After several months, Woit told Stevie to run around the gym. Stevie was incredulous. So were the six middle-aged men, including two doctors, exercising in the room.

But Stevie began the painful trek, stumbling, groaning, wobbling against the wall, being lashed onward by Woit's reedy voice. "You'll never do it, you bum." Stevie went down one side, then across the gym, then finally back up.

As he excruciatingly neared the exercise room the six men watching with tears in their eyes began to quietly applaud.

Then the men returned to their class, one of eight Woit daily conducts. It is a 40-minute regimen of situps, pushups, weightlifts, and sprints. Faster, faster; many, more. Woit does everything along with them to gain their respect.

In order for his body to accept such activity, Woit had to lose nearly 50 pounds, going from a solid 170 pounds on his 5-foot-7 frame to a solid—it's true—120 pounds. He rarely eats a full meal and seems to survive nicely on fruit juices, vitamin pills and, his vice, candy bars.

The men in his class range from businessmen to pro athletes. They include men who first came up because they were overweight or overwrought or ailing.

Gale Sayers, once the great running back of the Chicago Bears, had come to Woit after suffering his first knee injury in 1968. Sayers credits Woit with helping him return to football the following season, in which he led the NFL in rushing.

Bob Love and Chet Walker of the Chicago Bulls basketball team have gone through the Woit route, as well as Dick Gordon, Bobby Douglass, and George Seals of the Bears.

Once, Sayers brought up Willie Davis, then all-pro defensive end for the Green Bay Packers. Davis, bending and lifting beside graying businessmen, lasted only part of the way. He had to run out the rear door onto the conveniently placed fire escape, where he vomited.

Woit, 42, was himself a pro football player, with the Detroit Lions in 1954 and 1955, until he suffered a concussion that ended his running back career. He never forgot, though, how important physical conditioning is, especially when you're a small pro.

He realized he could do more than anyone expected of him. He learned how to push himself. And by extension, others.

He went to the University of Chicago where he received a master's degree in physical therapy. He should also have gotten one in psychology, according to the men who take his class.

"His technique is unusual," said Paul Lapping, a meat trader, "he knows just how far to push a man."

A fellow we will call Lennie, age 62, was brought by his brother-in-law to Woit last year. Lennie had had a stroke and now dragged along now with a cane and spoke in barely audible mutterings.

Woit, as he does with all his "heart attack guys" and "cancer guys" and "lung operation guys" and "crips," among others, took a warm if typically camouflaged interest in Lennie. When a guy doesn't show up for a couple days—even if he must travel, like Lennie, 100 miles overall to get to the gym—Woit solicitiously calls their home to check on their well-being. ("But I don't want that to get out," said Woit. "My image, you know.")

Woit began to walk Lennie around the gym, holding Lennie's cane, and sometimes striking him with it when Lennie instinctively reached out for the wall.

"I used to come home with welts on my side from Dick's

beating me with my cane," said Lennie, wearing a Woit's Warrior T-shirt. "But I started to walk right. I began to talk right. And I lost 30 pounds doing the exercises he prescribed. I'd leave the gym drooling with sweat. He changed my life, thank God."

Not long after Lennie began his exercises, Woit received a phone call at the gym. It was Lennie's wife. "Mr. Woit," she began, haltingly, "I don't know if this is proper. But I felt I had to tell you."

"What is it?" asked Woit.

"Last night, for the first time since before Len's illness, we were, well, we were husband and wife again."

Hard-bitten Dick Woit, the man with the sandpaper vocabulary, absorbed this for a moment, and then said, "I think that is the most beautiful thing I've ever heard."

Track Circus

Only a circus or carnival or a silent-film flatfoot chase can compare to an indoor track meet.

A merry-go-round of contortions, a kaleidoscope of colors, a dizzying Ferris wheel of highs and lows, an acrid odor of, say, horses and hay under the stands.

The ponderous man, in all his puff and heave, twirls like an elephant on one leg and delicately balances in one hand the shot, like a demitasse.

Crack of a gun. Or somebody suddenly clearing his throat harshly. Four ladies without the pawky gawkiness of girls careen around the track in the sprint medley relay. The leader's long blond hair sticks straight back in the breeze like a shredded fusilage.

The other three are chasing her with thick implements, and she's got one of her own in case they catch her.

Crack of a gun. Or the midgets' rattletrap backfiring. And the hurdlers spilling out of the starting blocks, cracking over hurdles, tumbling over their feet, stumbling across the wire, barreling into the wall, crawling up the red protective mat. Bursting if they win.

In the infield, in sweat pants and sweat jacket and sweat socks and seriously sweaty brow, a dash man does the bicycle on his back, kicking like a flipped-over fly; a triple-jump man struts in place like a frustrated majorette; a high-jumper bounds about wearing floppy hat and carrying an umbrella.

In the infield, too, is a vaulter dragging his pole as an ant does with a new-found treasure twig, and one high-hurdles gal, sumptuous tresses, touching her toes, impersonates an old English sheepdog.

Up, up above, flitting from ceiling light to ceiling light like a moth, is a man on a solitary stilt. Magically, the pole vaulter halts high in midair, encompassing eternity for a moment, then drops down from the electric-light sky. If only he had a unicycle he could change the stars for greater wattage and clown a little, too.

Crack of a gun. A rocket take off, fizzing slowly, and the long-distance runners, with miles to go before they sleep, with miles to go before they sleep, ease into a wary trot, barely a trot.

Here, coming down the runway, the long jumper is loping. Then he leaps with long, veiny legs and arms outstretched as if to catch the hands of his trapeze partner.

The officials stuffed in tuxedos study the long-jumpers' footprints in the sawdust, looking like Mr. Sherlock Holmes without magnifying glass, though a monocle might fit; a strain of necks at the high-jump bar; a squint at a stopwatch, a scowl at a disappointing time; a yawn by a fan.

And is there anything more humorous and painful to

watch than the one-mile walk? Unless it be a turtle race. Or a clown trying to sweep a spotlight circle under a mat in center ring. The walkers walk: no-nonsense heels-and-toes and elbows, determined chins dug deep into chests, an angry shimmy of hips.

"Look," shouts a boy in the stands, laughing and pointing, "look at that small shrimp lagging behind." The shrimp finished the walk, alone, and to hell with everyone else is written on his glasses-and-grimaced face.

But now it is over. Sweat hangs heavy in the air. The fun is silenced. It is quiet, except for the blank-faced, heavy-lidded workers. They arrive to fold away neatly the poles, mats, hurdles. They go about their task like embalmers.

The Box Score Lives!

The baseball box score is older than the game itself—the professional game, that is—more durable than any single game and sometimes more enthralling. The box score is so awesome it has been deemed "a document of history," so enchanting to be tendered "an urban flower," so informative as to be called "a form of telegraphy," and so bewitching it is known as "a kind of black art."

All this from a seemingly cold, intellectual, small printed box of names and numbers, lined up in columns, sprinkled with apostrophes and dots and commas and fractions; yet it is as emotional as an impressionist painting or a booming symphony, producing hope, dread, joy, and depression, depending where the heart of the reader is. The box score is a marvel. It is to baseball what the invention of the wheel has been to civilization, at least.

The box score is something you wake up to. You read to see who did what, how the game went. It can be savored all day long. Without ever having watched the game, one knows the tenor and tempo from these rows of type. Baseball, it seems, lends itself more readily to statistics than any other sport. It is linear, arithmetical, and highly individual. It is also hopelessly nostalgic.

"We American men," said author James T. Farrell, "are a nation of frustrated baseball players, and the literature of our childhood was play-by-play, morning-after stories and box scores. These box scores, in the days of our boyhood, read like documents of history."

Baseball and summer are virtually synonymous. And when Roger Angell, New Yorker writer, noted one wintry New York February morning the arrival of Florida spring training in his newspaper, he wrote, "now spring is guaranteed and one of my favorite urban flowers, the baseball box score, will burgeon and flourish through the warm, languid, information-packed weeks and months just ahead."

No general statement, no vague fog of a thought is the box score. A whiff is a whiff. A hit is a hit. "A bloop looks the same as a line drive in the box score," is the saying of ballplayers.

The men in the field are as entranced with the box scores as are the fans. It is their telegraphic system. They do reconaissance on rivals. Who is hot at the plate? Who is throwing hard? "Gr'b'r'w'tz is 2-for-4, 3-for-5 and 2-for-5," notes an opposing manager. "But he's been swinging against righties. We'll have to feed him lefties."

Something comforting, too, in the box score's known limits. All 130,000 batters in a season are accounted for. All pitchers are responsible for their actions.

To the statistician—and a baseball fan *must* be a statistician of sorts—the box score is a never-ending waterfall of information. "It's an exact science, as opposed to the game," said Seymour Siwoff, head of the Elias Statistical Bureau in New York.

The box score was created, mysteriously enough, by a man known only from his initials, F.W.T. In 1853 he sent a rudimentary numerical account of the game to a paper in New York called "The Spirit of the Times." It grew and was improved upon by Henry Chadwick, one of the earliest baseball chroniclers. One of his items was "hands left," which meant "outs."

The glories of the box score grew to 11 columns by 1880. And one bookkeeper in Brooklyn had as many as 70 items, from number of hits to number of linear feet run on these hits.

Modest changes in this by now hallowed tradition have been proposed through the years. But of course few were made. Then in 1968 the wire services decided to drop things like assists and putouts and specifics on pinch-hittters. The reasoning was that with so many new teams, and new sports, box scores were taking up too much newspaper space. There was an outcry: "Blasphemy!" Dyed-in-the-boxes fans would sooner eliminate the game stories.

Once you could tell if the pitching was high or low, depending on the putouts; if outfielders were getting many it meant the pitcher was throwing high. This intelligence was eliminated with "P" and "A." Also cut out were the names of the double-play participants. This pained the box-score reader, too.

To save even more space, some newspapers have been running nothing more than the line scores. That is a cold-coffee-and-hard-bread diet for baseball buffs.

Some feel that the future of the box score is at stake, that a victim of "modern progress" is being prepared for execution.

"People must realize," said Siwoff, "that the box score is immortal. Oh, what a treasure would be lost!"